The Mystery of Christ and the Apostolate

THE MYSTERY OF
CHRIST AND THE
APOSTOLATE

F.-X. Durrwell

Translated by Edward Quinn

Sheed and Ward · London and New York

First published 1972

Sheed and Ward Inc, 64 University Place, New York, N.Y. 10003, and
Sheed and Ward Ltd, 33 Maiden Lane, London WC2E 7LA

This book is a translation of the chapters 1–8 of
Le mystère pascal, source de l'apostolat,
les Editions Ouvrières, Paris 1970.

Nihil obstat: John M. T. Barton, STD LSS, *Censor*
Imprimatur: † Victor Guazzelli, *Vicar General*
Westminster, 17 January 1972

Library of Congress Catalog Number: 72–1482

This book is set in 11 on 13pt Baskerville type
Made and printed in Great Britain
by W & J Mackay Limited, Chatham

CONTENTS

ABBREVIATIONS

CBQ	*Catholic Biblical Quarterly*, Washington 1939–
CCL	*Corpus Christianorum, Series Latina*, Turnhout 1953–
CSEL	*Corpus Scritorum Ecclesiasticorum Latinorum*, Vienna 1875–
DS	*Enchiridion Symbolorum, Definitionum et Declarationum de Rebus Fidei et Morum*, ed. H. Denzinger, revised edition by A. Schönmetzer, Freiburg 1963
Eph Theol. Lov.	*Ephemerides Theologicae Lovanienses*, Bruges 1924–
GSS	*Die griechischen christlichen Schriftsteller der ersten Jahrhunderte*, Berlin 1899–
NTS	*New Testament Studies*, Cambridge 1954–
PG	*Patrologiae Cursus completus, Series Graeca*, ed J. P. Migne, Paris 1857–
PL	*Patrologiae Cursus completus, Series Latina*, ed. J. P. Migne, Paris 1844–
Rech. Sc. Rel.	*Recherches de Science religieuse*, Paris 1910–
TDNT	*Theological Dictionary of the New Testament*, ed. G. Kittel and G. Friedrichs, Grand Rapids, Michigan, 1964– (translation of *Theologisches Wörterbuch zum Neuen Testament*, Stuttgart 1930–)

The documents of the Second Vatican Council are referred to by short titles as follows:

Bishops Decree on the Bishops' Pastoral Office in the Church (*Christus Dominus*)

The Church Dogmatic Constitution on the Church (*Lumen Gentium*)

Church in the Modern World Pastoral Constitution on the Church in the Modern World (*Gaudium et Spes*)

Ecumenism Decree on Ecumenism (*Unitatis Redintegratio*)

Laity Decree on the Apostolate of the Laity (*Apostolicam Actuositatem*)

Liturgy Constitution on the Sacred Liturgy (*Sacrosanctum Concilium*)

Missions Decree on the Church's Missionary Activity (*Ad Gentes*)

Priestly Formation Decree on Priestly Formation (*Optatam Totius*)

Priests Decree on the Ministry and Life of Priests (*Presbyterorum Ordinis*)

Religious Freedom Declaration on Religious Freedom (*Dignitatis Humanae*)

Religious Life Decree on the Appropriate Renewal of the Religious Life (*Perfectae Caritatis*)

Revelation Dogmatic Constitution on Divine Revelation (*Dei Verbum*)

PREFACE

Whenever a new book appears, it is expected to be relevant to the issues of its time. But does it therefore have to give an absolutely fresh answer to present-day queries? Novelty is not necessarily progress. If a problem has once been given a correct answer—even though this has often been forgotten in the meantime—why not propose it yet again in its eternal truth?

The apostolate has always raised problems—very serious problems—for the church: they touch her very life and present themselves today in a singularly acute form. It is certainly not an exaggeration to say that the crisis of the church is primarily a crisis of the apostolate. Doesn't it appear with special virulence among christians concerned about the apostolate and above all among those who more than the rest are appointed as apostles, among priests?

The purpose of the present book, devoted to a theological study of the apostolate, is to create a better understanding of an answer to present-day questions, an answer given long ago. God has spoken and still speaks in Jesus Christ. Must a book lack timeliness because it is at the service of the eternal Word? Anyone who flatters himself on being up to date should take care, for time passes quickly: 'Novelty grows old more rapidly than anything else in the world' (C. Valéry). People sometimes think that the gospel no longer counts today: in fact, it belongs to tomorrow; it is the future which the church must try to acclimatize in the present. It alone remains young forever.

Scripture however is explicit. It proclaims that God accomplishes men's salvation in Jesus Christ, that he evangelizes them in Jesus Christ. Whatever may be said, there exists a 'soul of the whole apostolate': union with Christ in his mystery of salvation.

THE MYSTERY OF GOD AND
THE APOSTOLATE*

We used to sing at Sunday vespers: *Quis sicut Deus noster qui in altis habitat?* 'Who is like our God who dwells on high?' The word *altum* means height, but also depth. Might we not also translate: 'Who is like our God who dwells in the depths?' An incomparable God, whose greatness would lie in infinite depth.

For physical science there are two infinities: that of immensity, the exterior infinity of unlimited space, and an infinity of littleness and unfathomable interiority, that of matter at its first origin, in its inaccessible depth. Of the two infinities the second is undoubtedly the more wonderful, the infinity of littleness.

God dwells on high, his power is exalted above us and above all things, according to the image of him suggested by the immensity of infinite space. But is there not also in God another dimension which must be conceived in the form of a descent to the very bottom of things, refraining from any assertion of this universal dominion, when God appears utterly discreetly—without seeming to do so—at the origin of all things?

The paradoxical greatness of God

When God revealed himself in the burning bush, he gave himself a name of incomparable greatness: 'I AM WHO I AM' (Ex 3:14). The faithful of the Old Testa-

---

* This chapter first appeared in *Masses ouvrières*, 258 (1969), 27-39.

ment worshipped the majesty of this name: 'The Lord
on high is mighty!' (Ps 93:4). But were they able to
form a true idea of this greatness? The child acquires the
notion of greatness and power by looking at his father.
He has to raise his eyes to see his father's face. His father
seems so big and strong: his strength may even frighten
the child. The Old Testament was an age of religious
infancy. Speaking about that time, St Paul says: 'When
we were children' (Gal 4:3). Man projected on to God
his own ideas of greatness, extending them to infinity:
the idea that the father inspires in the child, that kings
try to inspire in their subjects. God is greater and stronger than all men. He was invoked as 'Great King!',
'Mighty King!', 'God of Armies!'.

It was perhaps in order to avenge this God of super-
human strength that Paul in his youth persecuted the
Christians whose crucified Messiah seemed to him an
outrage to the power of God and the hope of Israel.
It is against this God of encroaching power that many
atheists revolt, fearing that an infinitely great and powerful God will leave no scope either for their existence or
for their freedom: 'Deliver us from a God who prevents us from being!'

This too is the God that we often worship, in a
humility which reduces us to nothing before him: for we
think that he wants to make us bend under his power,
acknowledging his majesty and our nothingness. And
yet, it was by drawing us out of nothing that God willed
us to be! God is the Other that man cannot conceive:
his greatness is different. The God of infinite power is
in fact Father of this crucified Jesus whom Paul persecuted in the name of God's power; it was in the death of
Christ that the eternal divine greatness was revealed.

God revealed in the mystery of the redemption

No man has known God in his profound truth, for he cannot be seen except in the redeeming Christ. 'Why dost thou hide thy face?' cried the psalmist. God's face was unveiled when Jesus in his death was seen to be the Son of God.

Of course we cannot conceive God's greatness in the same way as man's. Since man is created in God's image, God is in some sense anthropomorphous. Man's countenance is forever the best revelation of God. But, alongside power in man, is there not also weakness, the disarming frankness of innocence and tenderness? Alongside the father's imposing stature, is there not the charm of infancy, alongside virile strength, maternal devotion and humility? All this is part of man's greatness. There even exist riches in humanity which are scarcely developed except in poverty and suffering. And it is in his death that man can attain his supreme greatness. Is there not in God something more than greatness imposing itself by strength, that more wonderful greatness which becomes apparent in the immolation of a loving heart? Is there in him nothing corresponding to this depth to which man rises by suffering and in the absolute weakness of his death?

God was formerly revealed in a fragmentary way (Heb 1:1), as in an image broken up into parts, as in a light decomposed by a prism. Men had taken one of the fragments which spoke of power and wanted to see in this fragment the whole image of God: in a single ray of the prism they thought they had discovered all the richness of divine light. But in Jesus Christ this light is revealed as in its first source. Never before had there appeared in the world the true man, created in the perfection of the divine resemblance. Christ dead and raised up is the true 'countenance of God',[1] revealed to the world. As Father of Jesus Christ, God is christomorphous: 'He who has seen me has seen the Father' (Jn 14:9).

Jesus foretold that men would fix their gaze on the image of God that he himself was to be on the day of his exaltation on the cross, as the Israelites had looked to the serpent raised up above the earth (Jn 3:14–15). He asked to be glorified in the paschal mystery, so as to be able to spread the knowledge of God (Jn 17:1–3). 'In that day (the eternal day of the paschal mystery) I shall no longer speak to you in figures but tell you plainly of the Father' (Jn 16:25). On the cross and in glory, 'he who shall see me shall see the Father himself.' For it is when he is glorified in his immolation that Jesus appears in the full truth of his sonship, 'designated Son of God in power' (Rom 1:4) in the mystery of the redemption. It is then that he is the burning bush of the supreme revelation: 'When you have lifted up the Son of man, then you will know that I am he' (Jn 8:28); he becomes 'the image of the invisible God' (Col 1:15) when, after death, he reaches the peak of the mystery of the incarnation, the 'reflection of the glory of God and bearing the very stamp of his nature' (Heb 1:3; 2 Cor 4:4). *Ecce homo*! Here is the man, the Son of God, the eternal image of his greatness. It is on a face first marked by blows, then covered with blood during the hours of agony, and in a body pierced through, that the truth of God is revealed. Christ will remain eternally what the cross made him, simultaneously immolated and glorified; the exal-

[1] The expression is that of Clement of Alexandria, speaking of the logos. Cf. *The Pedagogue* I, 7 (P.G.8, 520).

tation of Christ will not go beyond the movement that raises him on the cross: it is there, in his immolation, that he is glorified. As St John puts it, the cross is the eternal throne of his glory.[1] Christians have always climbed and to the end of time will climb this mountain of contemplation in order to see Christ in his truth: 'They shall look on him whom they have pierced' (Jn 19:37).

Henceforward the cross is erected at all the crossroads of humanity, the tree of knowledge where man can learn the science of the true God. Following the example of the apostle Thomas, Christians kneel down and worship the greatness of God when they see the wounds of the risen Christ: 'My Lord and my God!' (Jn 20:28).

The paschal mystery makes God's humility visible

Finally revealed as far as he possibly can be, God appears more mysterious than ever in this paschal Christ whose face is covered with opprobrium and glory, the Lamb who is standing and at the same time slain (Rev 5:6), in whom the contraries form a single unity: the omnipotence of the risen one and the total weakness of his death. *In this image of God the divine being is expressed simultaneously by these two extremes: power and weakness, universal lordship and absolute humility.*

Death and life are not parallel realities in the paschal Christ, but combined, even identified, distinct only for our mind. In Revelation (5:5) Christ is proclaimed as the Lion of Judah who has gained the victory, and yet he appears as a little lamb slain. He is shepherd of the immense flock; but, as the Lamb, he is the smallest of the

---

[1] According to St John (cf 12:32–36) Christ's exaltation above the earth to the presence of the Father is accomplished within the mystery of his death.

flock, made great in his immolation (cf Rev 7:14, 17). In order to know the greatness of God, our mind must therefore move in two apparently opposite directions: to the heights and to the depths, to omnipotence which places God infinitely above us and to his refusal to assert his own power before us; we have to follow these opposite extremes to the end and reduce them to unity. For we shall never know God in his truth unless we contemplate him in the paschal Christ *in whom infinite power means absolute immolation.*

This is not to say that there is weakness and littleness in God as these exist in men, any more than power is in him as it is conceived by men, for 'the weakness of God is stronger than men' (1 Cor 1:25). But, translated into the human language of the incarnation, God's mode of being is expressed both in the humility of the death of Christ and in the omnipotence of his glory. For *God is love and his omnipotence is nothing other than his infinite love,* and we know that real love is always humble, and always sacrifices itself for the loved one. There is an incomprehensible mystery of divine humility and of immolation, humility and immolation in their absolute purity, prerogative of eternal love.

God's greatness lies in the humility of his self-giving. Already, while he was on earth, Jesus had conveyed this image of God as a being of that sovereign greatness which is the humility of self-giving. He calls himself 'the true shepherd,' attributing to himself a name of greatness formerly reserved to God as guide and protector of Israel (Ezek 34:11f.; Ps 80:1). Not only is he called *a* true shepherd, but *the* true shepherd, the only one there is, the universal shepherd. Nevertheless, he claims this divine title only because of the self-giving which he is going to accomplish and because of the humility of his death: 'I am the good shepherd. The good shepherd lays down his life' (Jn 10:11). He also calls himself 'the bread of life' (Jn 6:35), a title which God alone can claim, for he alone can feed the whole world, feed it for eternal life. But it is in the extreme humility and love shown in his death that he reaches this greatness: 'the bread which I shall give for the life of the world is my flesh' (Jn 6:51). Flesh given, bread eaten: how strange is the greatness of divinity!

On Palm Sunday God anticipates by a week Christ's entry into the kingdom. On that day all things give way to the action of God glorifying Jesus, and the very stones would cry out if men were silent (Lk 19:40). This divine power is revealed, however, not in a show of strength, but in a humble tenderness: 'Tell the daughter of Zion, Behold, your king is coming to you, humble' (Mt 21:5). For God's glory is that of infinite love. Sweet and humble is the heart of Christ and gentle the yoke of his dominion.

Because he is the Son of God, in the image of his Father, Jesus is poor on earth, poorer than the bird and the fox, the prince of the 'poor of Yahweh'. He is disarmed in the presence of the powerful ones of this world; he identifies himself with those who are naked, hungry and thirsty, with the least among his brethren. He takes the initiative, goes first to meet the other, forgives, is ready to forgive seventy times seven times; he is not a superman, he is sensitive to joy, sensitive to gratitude; injustice and suffering crush him.

On the eve of his passion Jesus washes the feet of his disciples, a gesture which is a sign, like the entry into Jerusalem: an anticipation of the purification of the world which he is going to accomplish in the paschal mystery. This slave's service—so servile that a Jewish master could demand it of a pagan, but not of a Jewish slave—Jesus does not regard as a humiliation: *he performs it with the intention of achieving a work of eternal greatness*, one which corresponds to his dignity as Son of God: 'Knowing that the Father had given all things into his hands, and that he had come from God and was going to God . . ., he began to wash the disciples' feet' (Jn 13:3–5). He reaches his supreme filial greatness in supreme humility, at one and the same time.

To eternity he will remain in this humility and in this greatness, both 'the greater' and 'the one who serves' (Lk 22:27; cf 12:37). Jesus had advised his disciples to take the last place if they were invited to a feast; then the master of the house would be able to say: 'Come up higher!' The parable as it stands does not mean that the person who takes the last place is in fact occupying the first. But in the feast of the kingdom Jesus is raised forever to the first place, because of the fact that he 'took the last place in such a way that no one can deprive him of it,'[1] *that place in the world which God alone is able to occupy*. Having washed the feet of his disciples and accepted death in advance, Jesus declares: 'Now is the Son of man glorified' (Jn 13:31).

For such is the greatness and glory of God, such is divine power, so little resembling the idea that men form of power and glory. Such is our God: he is Father of Jesus Christ, of this Jesus Christ in utter weakness, given up for the life of the world. Whatever he possesses, Jesus has from his Father (Jn 8:28): this love and this

---

[1] The phrase is that of Fr Huvelin, often repeated by Charles de Foucauld. Cf J.-Fr. Six, *Itinéraire spirituel de Charles de Foucauld*, Paris 1958, pp. 79, 182, 217.

humility he draws from the love and humility of his Father. The mystery of sonship reaches its consummation in his death: in it Jesus 'goes to his Father', he becomes 'the only Son, who is in the bosom of the Father' (Jn 1:18), because he rejoins the Father in dying to himself. The Father then recognizes in him his own image, his beloved Son: 'For this reason the Father loves me, because I lay down my life, that I may take it again' (Jn 10:17).

A GOD WHO MAKES A GIFT OF HIS GLORY

The atheist demanded: 'Deliver us from a God who prevents us from being!' He can be reassured: the power of God in Jesus Christ does not crush anyone. A poor, humble person does not crush anyone. It is his infinite being that gives us our existence, his omnipresence which secures the space we need, his supreme freedom that creates ours. The God of infinite greatness, our creator, makes us a gift of his greatness: 'I have given you the kingdom, the power, the glory' (Dan 2:37) and freedom. His true image is that of the shepherd who gives his life so that the sheep 'may have life, and have it abundantly' (Jn 10:10).

A theological axiom states that God creates for his glory, seeks his glory in everything. This is true, but he does not pursue his glory as men work for theirs: the glory proper to God is the giving of glory, of not exalting himself before the creature but of exalting the creature; he acts always in accordance with the purity of his being, which is the gift of himself.[1]

[1] God however does not deprive himself of his glory, as the 'death of God' theology suggests: he imparts it and thus asserts and reveals his glory.

A redeeming God

From all these facts there emerges a truth on which it is particularly important to dwell, which is bewildering for our ways of thinking and even more for our ways of feeling: at the origin of creation, at the beginning and at the centre, in all God's dealings with us, there is a mystery which corresponds to the death of Christ for men's salvation. Everything had to begin and everything does begin unceasingly in the mystery of the redemption, since, in his glorifying death, Christ is the complete revelation of God's being in his relations with men. *The mystery of creation is part of the mystery of redemption.*[1]

[1] This basic truth throws a great deal of light on the world: humble, obscure light, similar to this truth itself, illuminating not in order to make things comprehensible, but to portend and hint at the meaning. It is a light thrown on the problem of evil, the evil of sin and that of suffering. If the power of God were similar to that of men, dominating, extended to infinity, no doubt there would be no sin in the world. But God's omnipotence is the omnipotence of love, both immolated and sovereign. Infinite love and infinite humility make hatred and pride possible.

The fact of suffering in the world, vast suffering, raises a still more insoluble problem. Yet Christians who have suffered much have found the solution of the problem; they have found it, not on the plane of their intelligence but existence. For them, even extraordinary suffering was not an intolerable absurdity. By bearing suffering in love, they did not feel that they were plunging into absurdity but finding the truth about themselves, in the union of their existence with God. Suffering and death are not unrelated to the God of whom Christ is the revelation; God carries in himself a mystery which in the man Jesus is called suffering and death. It is possible therefore to see suffering and death as a necessary part of the creation and divinisation of men until this divinisation reaches its term in a glory which will not reject death, but 'absorb it' into itself.

This again means that redemption is not merely the granting of forgiveness, not only the blotting out of sin, but the work of creation in which God leads man to his fullness by making him the gift of his glory.

The christian duty of being for others

Born of the revelation made in his redemptive death, Christianity is the religion of redeeming love. There lies its truth and its greatness. God imparts to his church that greatness which, in Christ, is the gift of himself for men's salvation. It is said (Eph 1:22–23) that the church is raised with Christ to the summit of all things: this means that she descends with him 'into the lower parts of the earth' (Eph 4:9), in the mystery of his death for the salvation of all. Being a christian, being in communion with Christ and sharing his divine sonship, means *living in Christ by dying with him for men's salvation*. It is in the redemptive mystery that God is adored by Christ and men, lived by them, imitated by them; the great christian liturgy is that of the redemption accomplished by Christ and by those who are united with him. At the centre of christian worship is the mass, where God is honoured, because the mystery of God is celebrated there and proclaimed within our world by the redemptive death of Christ and because we take part in it for the salvation of men. The new commandment is to love by giving one's life (cf. Jn 15:12–13), giving it not to be annihilated—for in God this love is power and the source of infinite life—but giving it in order to live and be the source of life.

The duty of the apostolate and the desire for the apostolate which animate the church, the testimony, the urgent supplication and endurance of trials, the offering of their life and their death which some christians make for the salvation of the world: all this is essential, all this has eternal roots and is part of the 'mystery which was kept secret for long ages, but is now disclosed' in Christ and in the church (Rom 16:25–26).

The duty of loving God

The christian can draw this redeeming love, which makes his greatness, only from the eternal source. He will love God and not indulge in stupid talk: 'God died in Jesus Christ; he has himself released us from his hold, from his religion; we have to be concerned only with the men for whom Christ died.' On the contrary, he will say: 'More than ever, God must be loved in Jesus Christ, with all our heart and all our strength, and—as the commandment requires—all the time; he must be loved with love and tenderness, since, in Jesus Christ, we have discovered that God is immolated.' The holiest christians have wanted to be with God even to the point of identifying themselves with him in that 'dying of love' of which they often speak. It is, moreover, in God alone that human love has the power to rebound on others for eternal life. It is going to his Father, in a love unto death (cf Jn 14:31), that Christ becomes saviour of men.

The duty of humility

Early writers said that humility is 'the mark of chris- tians'.[1] It is easy to believe them when christianity is regarded as the divinisation of the world and a mis- sionary religion, and the church as sacrament of salva-

[1] Cf Pseudo-Macarius, *Hom.* 15 and 26 (*PG* 34, 593, 681); Hesychius, *De Temperantia et Virtute, Cent* 1 (*PG* 93, 1505).

tion for all. The christian will have to follow Christ and choose the lowest place in the world, that of Christ the saviour and that of God, the place of total service.

God does not require humility of the christian in order to humiliate him, to constrain him to avow his nothingness and bow down before the divine majesty. The christian is the child of God. What father would be so foolish as to require his son to kneel at his feet? *God demands humility in order to raise man to his own level*, making him share the riches of his love. The sign of the cross, that sign of humility which the christian makes on himself, is the mark of his sonship. The place of Christ in the world, this last place chosen in love, is, in spite of appearances, that of the Lord of the universe.

Over and over again scripture requires the faithful to become like God, 'perfect, as your heavenly Father is perfect' (Mt 5:48). 'Be imitators of God,' says St Paul (Eph 5:1). In current speech it is not a commendation of a person's humility and readiness to serve, to say, 'He behaves as if he were God.' This is the language that St Paul uses of Christ's adversary, 'who exalts himself, proclaiming himself to be God' (2 Thess 2:4). But, in face of the Father of Jesus Christ, a God of pride and domination would be the very opposite of God. Being perfect in the way our Father in heaven is perfect means being indulgent, humble, to the point of forgiving unceasingly: 'Love your enemies, so that you may be sons of your Father who is in heaven' (Mt 5:44–45); 'be kind to one another, tender-hearted, forgiving one another, as God in Christ forgave you. Therefore be imitators of God, as beloved children. And walk in love, as Christ loved us and gave himself up for us' (Eph 4:32–5:2).

The Gospel for the Poor[1]

'The sign of christianity' and of its greatness is also the humility of those to whom its message is addressed. It was this sign of the authenticity of the mission of Jesus that John the Baptist had to recognize. 'Are you he who is to come?' the Forerunner had asked. And Jesus had replied: 'Go and tell John what you hear and see . . . the poor have good news preached to them' (Mt 11: 3–5).

For God chooses the little ones to make his kingdom of them: 'Fear not, little flock, for it is your Father's good pleasure to give you the kingdom' (Lk 12:32). It is to them that he reveals himself, among them that he makes his glory dwell: 'I thank thee, Father, Lord of heaven and earth, that thou hast hidden these things from the wise and understanding and revealed them to babes: yea, Father, for such was thy gracious will' (Mt 11:25–26). The God of greatness, the 'Lord of heaven and earth,' reveals himself to the little ones. This is not a whim, it is his good pleasure, for he reveals himself to them in virtue of their affinity with him; he takes pleasure in giving himself to them. He appears to the one who is close to him, to the little man, to the simple, to the poor man who is God's neighbour, the first to be touched by his appeal: 'God chose what is foolish in the world, . . . what is weak, . . . what is low and despised in the world' (1 Cor 1:27–28).

In a language of love

To the poor God speaks the language of God. He speaks the language of the cross,[2] which is 'folly to those who

[1] *Church* 8; *Missions* 5; *Liturgy* 5.
[2] Cf *Missions* 5.

are perishing,' but to those who listen to it 'the power of God' (1 Cor 1:18). He does not raise his voice to compel people to hear; the appeal of faith 'springs from the weakness of God' and man is free to listen and to follow it; if he listens, it will be with the generosity of love, in 'that holy chivalry of the heart which flies to the defense of defenseless truth.'[1]

God spoke in this way through 'his servant whom he has chosen, . . . on whom he put his Spirit to proclaim justice to the Gentiles,' Christ who did not 'wrangle or cry aloud' and did not make 'his voice heard in the streets' (Mt 12:18-19). It is in this way too that God speaks through the apostles: 'I came to you proclaiming the testimony of God (to convey the testimony given by God himself), not in lofty words or wisdom. For I decided to know nothing among you except Jesus Christ and him crucified. And I was with you in weakness and in much fear, . . . that your faith might not rest in the wisdom of men but in the power of God' (1 Cor 2:1-5).

Undoubtedly the power that transcends all things can enter into our reality, remaining what it is, if not in littleness then in forms contrary to human power: 'power is made perfect in weakness' (2 Cor 12:9). A triumphalist church, of commanding power, could not be the presence of the God of greatness; her glory would be a sham. She must make herself heard in a language of love, which is a language of immolation, that of a queen who has been described as a servant and poor. She must

[1] R. Guardini, *The Lord*, London, New York, Toronto, 1956, p. 126: 'Faith requires not only the simple will to God's truth, but also a certain responsiveness to precisely this "weakness" of God . . . In truth's very defenselessness must lie an unspeakable mystery of love.'

not subject men to her domination, but put herself at the service of their freedom. Her mission is to invite men to freedom, for it is she who has to rouse the faith by which man, giving himself and all he has, commits himself totally for God and for men. For no act is freer than the total gift of self. Undoubtedly the church must 'preach the word, be urgent in season and out of season' (2 Tim 4:2), for she must love and love is passionate in its demands. But she must not force the truth on people:[1] Love seeks to create and not to dominate. Like God himself, it must accept reverses.

The duty of creating the apostolate

The apostle has not received any power to dominate, even within the church (cf 1 Cor 1:23–24). In the name of God's greatness, any clericalism is excluded from the definition of the apostolate. The apostle has power only to be a witness of the God revealed in Jesus Christ. 'If anyone would be first' in the church, 'he must be last of all' (Mk 9:35).

He would want to dominate if he claimed to be an apostle on his own, if he refused to share the apostolate with the community. Those whom God creates, he wants to be like himself: he is a creator of causes. In the world, God disappears behind the action of creatures; Christ has died and no longer acts himself in the world, he makes his followers act: he has died so that the church may be born and be the mother of men. The apostle therefore will raise up apostles, will share with them his powers and responsibilities; he will know how to die so that others may act; he will know how to act with power by dying to himself. So those who are first in the

[1] Cf *Missions* 13; *Religious Freedom* 10; *Revelation* 5.

church will be the servants of all by making them apostles.

We are true, adult christians only when we are apostles. But, in order to make christians, someone else must always die, someone must die to himself.

Reading the scriptures we see the true image of God taking shape, gradually and very slowly. The light of the divine countenance is more and more interiorised, transcendence is revealed as intimacy; God's action, at first imposed as from outside, becomes in the faithful an immanent life and strength becomes love. The features of a merely external resemblance to man become blurred and, when God comes to reveal himself completely in a man, it is in this man's death that he is revealed. At its final stage evolution does not disown its starting point, for progress means gaining in depth: the term is revealed as being what was always the beginning, the deeper explanation of the first manifestations.

God 'mighty on high' and God who, at the term, is revealed in Jesus Christ, who has descended into the lower parts of the earth in death, where he fills all things (Eph 4:9–10). God so much the greater, more inaccessible and more completely pure power! This evolution of divine revelation is parallel to the history of salvation, progressing from the fringe of reality to a profound fullness, from the first creation accomplished in power to a final creation in the love that contains the first.

It is in the depths that the church can gain access to the resources accumulated in Christ for this final creation. There is a law which states that power is directly proportionate to depth. By penetrating to the interior of the structures of matter, modern man has been able to release energies which are in no way proportionate to the physical or chemical forces at the surface. This law of depth, which governs matter, is even more the law of christian existence and activity. The church must descend to her very depths, to where she is the church of God: in the glorifying death of Christ, where the Lord is given to her and she is given to the Lord. The faith which makes the christian die to himself and the deep prayer which scripture says should be unceasing, true fraternal service and the unity of ecclesial charity with the renunciations it involves, the courage of a totally evangelical life and the pure, divine charity that so many christians nourish in themselves in so many trials: all these are realities in which God's saving power never ceases to break through to the world. This power is in the world where the world is itself in God: in the death of Christ.

In the fourth gospel Jesus calls himself 'the door of the sheep' (10:7), the door which gives access to the sheep, through which the apostles come and go. All those who want to enter by another door are thieves (v.8). But the Christ of whom the text speaks is the good shepherd who gives his life: he is the door of the apostolate in his glorifying death.

2

CREATION AND THE APOSTOLATE*

The relations between God and men could be conceived as different from what they are and the salvation effected by Christ understood in such a way that it would not constitute God's basic project. For some centuries now christian thought has been dominated by a theology which, although centred on the death of Christ—but on this alone—did not place this death at the heart of human existence. It was a theology of sin and its expiation: it taught that the plan of redemption had come to renew God's creative plan, impaired by Adam's sin, or had been added on to the original plan. In his very depths, at his creation, therefore, man did not depend on the love of God as manifested in the redeeming Christ: salvation in Christ did not involve man's whole existence, down to his very roots.

In such a perspective the apostolate is at the service of a work of reparation, its aim being to distribute the forgiveness obtained by Christ, to restore the work disturbed by sin. Since it cannot reach man at his roots, neither can the ministry involve the apostle in his most personal existence: he can be no more than a means for the distribution of forgiveness and grace.

All reflection on the apostolate comes up against this problem of the relations between creation and redemption, human values and christian values. Numerous

* This chapter is an expanded version of a study which appeared in *Bible et Vie chrétienne* 54 (1963), 16–28.

questions arise, the most insistent being undoubtedly that of the salvation of human beings who are not touched by the church's preaching. In order to answer this question theology must start by trying to rise to as accurate as possible an appreciation of these relations. According to Vatican II, Christ's salvation, mediated by the church, involves the whole man, 'man himself, whole and entire';[1] the council thinks that 'only in the mystery of the incarnate Word does the mystery of man take on light'[2] and, to prove this, quotes a pauline text (Col 1:15)[3] which places man's creation within the mystery of Christ.

I—GOD CREATES IN CHRIST

From his conversion onwards, St Paul never stopped proclaiming Christ the Lord. At Colossae strange doctrines were trying to gain ground at the expense of this unique lordship, placing between God and men mediating 'powers', 'thrones' and 'principalities', to which homage had to be paid by 'self-abasement' (Col 2:18). In the face of these theories, the apostle reasserts the redemptive lordship of Christ, proving that it is unique and absolute, that it extends to the very origin of things and to the dawn of history, for it is the lordship of God himself who, in Christ, creates the world (Col 1:13-20):[4]

[1] *Church in the Modern World* 3, 2.
[2] *Church in the Modern World* 22, 1.
[3] *Church in the Modern World* 22, 2.
[4] The author gives his own literal translation of this passage. But a translation from the French would have differed little from the RSV text which I have used. In v. 16 Fr Durrwell has *par lui et vers lui* and consistently uses *vers* throughout the chapter when speaking of creation as having its end (or final

¹³He has delivered us from the dominion of darkness and transferred us to the kingdom of his beloved Son,

> ¹⁴in whom we have redemption, the forgiveness of sins.

> > ¹⁵He is the image of the invisible God,
> > the first-born of all creation;
> > > ¹⁶for in him all things were created,
> > > in heaven and on earth,
> > > visible and invisible,
> > > whether thrones or dominions or
> > > principalities or authorities—
> > all things were created through him and
> > for him.
> > > ¹⁷He is before all things and in him all
> > > things hold together.
> > > ¹⁸He is the head of the body, the church;

> > he is the beginning,
> > the first-born from the dead,
> > > that in everything he might be pre-
> > > eminent.
> > > ¹⁹For in him all the fullness of God was
> > > pleased to dwell,
> > > ²⁰and through him to reconcile to himself
> > > all things,
> > > whether on earth or in heaven,
> > > making peace by the blood of his cross.

A question arises: who is this beloved Son, for whom the apostle claims such an absolute pre-eminence in the

---

cause) in Christ. In order to be consistent with RSV I have translated *vers* as 'for', which also seems the most suitable English word to convey the same sense. *Trans.*

work of creation as well as in that of the redemption? Is he the uncreated Word, considered apart from the incarnation, or in fact Christ, the man who is Son of God, the incarnate Word?

The reply seems obvious: when the Son of God entered history, creation had been completed and in fact a long time before: he could therefore have played the creative role attributed to him by the apostle only in his eternal existence, *outside* the mystery of the incarnation. The work of the redemption however belongs to the Son of God in his human existence. To the Word then belongs creative action, to Christ—that is, to the incarnate Word redemptive. This division of roles also seems to be suggested by the division of the text into two strophes, the first extolling principally the creative action of the Son of God and the other principally his work of redemption.

But this interpretation is demanded only by theological reasoning: it is based on the impossibility of Christ's exercising an activity prior to his historical existence. Scripture however must be interpreted, not in the light of theology, but in its own light: it is scripture that is the source of theology and, in order to understand it, the only decisive criterion is the text itself, read in its context and in the faith of the church.

The 'beloved Son' is Christ[1]

It has often been observed that, in St Paul, the Son of God and his action are never considered apart from his revelation to the world by the incarnation. There are moreover several other pauline texts which attribute

[1] Cf *The Church*, 2; *Revelation*, 2; *Church in the Modern World*, 10, 2; 22, 2.

to Christ an action in the world prior to his entry into history: 'the Rock (at Horeb) was Christ' (1 Cor 10:4):[1] already, at the time of the exodus, Christ played the part of the rock of Israel. 'The Lord', against whom the Israelites murmured (1 Cor 10:9), seems in fact in St Paul's thought to be the same Christ.[2] Finally, in 1 Corinthians 8:6, the apostle explicitly attributes to Christ a role in creation: 'one Lord, Jesus Christ, through whom are all things and through whom we exist.' There is then a context which justifies us in attributing to Christ a role in creation.[3] As for the text itself, it contains evidence clear enough to lead exegetes increasingly to interpret it as a whole with reference to Christ.

The two strophes are introduced by verses 13 and 14 and remain closely linked to these;[4] the sole subject of attribution of the roles of creator and redeemer is this 'beloved Son, in whom we have redemption, the forgiveness of sins'; it is he, this Son who is saviour, who 'is the image of the invisible God, in whom all things were created, who is the head of the body, the first-born from the dead.'[5] The thought of the author goes back, without a break, from Christ the saviour to Christ the creator.

[1] Paul does not say: 'The rock is Christ,' which would mean 'must be interpreted of Christ'. Independently of any interpretation, the rock *was* Christ.

[2] According to a variant which might be original we would have to read: 'Do not let us put Christ to the test.' There is a similar variant reading of Jude 5.

[3] Rev 3:14 provides a text very similar to Col 1:16. There Christ is called 'the beginning of God's creation'.

[4] B. Rigaux even suggests incorporating verses 13 to 14 in the hymn itself. *Saint Paul et ses lettres*, Bruges/Paris 1962, 193.

[5] It is difficult to believe that, in these closely linked verses, Saint Paul is constantly changing the subject, speaking sometimes of the Word alone, at others of the incarnate Word. Cf J. Bonsirven, *L'Evangile de Paul*, Paris 1948, 86.

The beloved Son, in whom everything is created, is *the image of the invisible God* (v.15). In Paul's eyes God dwells in inaccessible light (1 Tim 6:16; cf Jn 1:18);[1] he emerges from this impenetrability, unveils his face, only in Christ. On the Damascus road Paul came to know this God whom he had not hitherto known in all his truth: he recognized him as the Father of our Lord Jesus Christ.[2] The scales fell, his eyes were opened as he turned towards the Christ of glory (cf. 2 Cor 3:16–18). It is always Christ who is the revelation of the invisible God, the divine countenance shown to men. 'The knowledge of the glory of God' is read 'in the face of Christ' (2 Cor 4:6); the Christian gazes 'with uncovered face on the "glory of the Lord" (Jesus), the image *par excellence*' (2 Cor 3:18).[3] The 'earthly man' already was created in the likeness of God (Gen 1:26–28), but the 'heavenly man', Christ, is 'the likeness of God' (2 Cor 4:4) in its transcendent perfection. Wishing to 'renew us after the image of our creator' (Col 3:10), it is in the likeness of Christ that God predestines us (Rom 8:29).

The text speaks of the 'beloved Son, in whom we have redemption, *who* is the image of the invisible God'; the pauline theology of Christ as image of God requires us to give this relative pronoun its full significance: the image of the invisible God is this Christ in whom we have redemption. This beloved Son is also '*the first-born of all creation*'. The apostle does not say 'the first-born

---

[1] He would say the same of the Word within the mystery of God.
[2] As several texts show, this was the apostle's most staggering experience. Cf D. M. Stanley, *The Resurrection of Christ in Pauline Soteriology*, Rome 1961, 262.
[3] The translation is that of L. Cerfaux, *Christ in the Theology of St Paul*, Edinburgh and London/New York 1959, 436.

before all creation': he places him in some way at the beginning of creation and within creation.[1]

It would be going too far to say that the text can refer only to the man Jesus, that it is 'impossible not to make the first-born the first in a series, as it is written in Romans: "the first-born among many brethren".'[2] The first-born of all creation is a being outside any series: he is first because 'in him all things were created'; in the transcendent act of God, in which he takes part, he is 'before' and above creation. And yet he is not unrelated to it, he is tied to creation by the very priority he has over it. It seems in fact that the apostle—the pauline perspective is one thing, that of the fourth gospel another—knows the Son of God only by his intervention in the work of God, both creative and redemptive. In order to appreciate the complexity of this thought, it seems we must understand the Son who is 'first-born of all creation' not only as a man and not only as God, but as the Son who is the 'image of the invisible God'. In this sense he is the incomparable image and the first-born of creation both by his transcendence and by his immersion into our world.[3]

---

[1] The Jerusalem Bible has this note: 'It is as the incarnate God that Jesus is the "image of God", that is, his human nature was the visible manifestation of God who is invisible, and it is as such, in this concrete human nature, and as part of creation, that Jesus is called the "first-born of creation"— not in the temporal sense of having been born first, but in the sense of having been given the first place of honour.'

[2] J. Bonsirven, *op. cit.*, 87.

[3] A. Feuillet, *Le Christ, Sagesse de Dieu*, Paris 1966, p. 198, n.1, writes: 'As for the title of image of the invisible God, is it not a means of uniting here the transcendent and the human sense?' This is what D. M. Stanley thinks, when he writes: 'In the order of creation, he appears as "first-born before all

Again it is said of this beloved Son: 'all things were created through him and for him' (v.16). The splendour of this and similar assertions might seem incompatible with the reality of the incarnation. But is it any easier to refer them to the Word apart from the mystery of the Incarnation? We can understand that everything was created by the Word, but it would be difficult to see that everything was created for him: by what title would the Word within the Trinity be the special term of creation? On the other hand, there is nothing to be said against the creation of all things for Christ, in whom the world is recapitulated, is completed and finds its unity; moreover the two epistles to the Colossians and Ephesians assert this: 'He has made known to us the mystery of his will, according to his purpose which he set forth in Christ, . . . to unite all things in him' (Eph 1:9–10; cf Col 1:20).

We can understand likewise that all things were 'created in Christ' (v.16), if it is true, as the apostle will claim (Col 1:19; 2:9), that God has concentrated in him the 'fullness' of all reality and all the divine forces of creation and sanctification. If all reality is concentrated in him, all is created in him, as a participation in his fullness.

From v.18 onwards there can be no doubt that the text is concerned with the redeeming Christ. The part played by 'the first-born from the dead', head of the

---

creatures." As only-begotten Son, he is "first-born" with reference to the Father's eternal act of generation. His humanity, however, permits him to be ranked first among all creatures, since they have been created "in him, by him, for him." ' 'Carmenque Christo Quasi Deo Dicere . . .' in CBQ 20 (1958), 188.

church, reconciler of all parts of the world, is again of the cosmic order. The creative sweep of his action, described in the first part, is not reduced. The dominion over death that is proper to the redeeming Christ (v.18), according to pauline thought, belongs to the cosmic order (cf Phil 3:21); the reconciliation of all things in the blood of the cross belongs also to this order; the preeminence over the church (v.18) is not merely juridical or imposed by external force, as are earthly sovereignties: Christ exercises his dominion over the church as God does, in virtue of the divine fullness imparted to him (v.19), a fullness which confers on him God's sovereignty over the universe (cf Eph 1:19–23). But henceforward the work of creation is no longer described in its origin, as in the first strophe, but at the eschatological culmination to which 'the blood of the cross' raises it.[1]

The beloved Son is the Christ of glory

We shall be less surprised at Paul's saying that everything is created in Christ, who 'is before all things', if we remember that Christ is seen, not in his earthly existence, but in his eternal fullness of glory. It is this Christ whom Paul encountered on the Damascus road, it is he who becomes for the apostle the source of his knowledge of the world and of history (cf 2 Cor 5:16). Everything in our text speaks of the lordly glory of the risen one: the

[1] A. Feuillet, *op. cit.*, writes: 'Here we put our finger on one of the peculiarities of the hymn: cosmological perspectives and history of salvation are closely linked here; even if certain verses relate to the cosmic role of Christ and others to his redemptive function, from one end of the passage to the other it is always a question of the same divine, invisible person, the incarnate Son of God whose various prerogatives the author contemplates one by one.'

kingdom of light into which we have been transferred (v.13), the salvation and forgiveness that we have forever 'in him' (v.14),[1] and, above all, this radiant image of the invisible God that is precisely the Christ of glory: 'the gospel of the glory of Christ, who is the likeness of God' (1 Cor 4:4). In what follows the apostle clearly directs our attention to Christ's resurrection: 'He is the head of the body, . . . the first-born from the dead' (v.18). According to Ephesians 1:19-23, Christ in his glorification is raised to the pinnacle of the universe, he is Lord of these same powers and principalities which the epistle to the Colossians also shows to be subject to Christ.

St Paul provides the decisive reason for the pre-eminence of Christ over the church and the world: 'For in him all the fullness of God was pleased to dwell' (v.19). This word 'pleroma' describes the totality of power, creative and sanctifying, and undoubtedly also the totality of being that is in God and through him in the universe. God concentrated this totality in Christ, even in his body of glory (Col 2:9), when he gave him his own name which is above all things, raising him to the plane of his being and his action, to where God is Lord (Phil 2:9-11). But God's dominion is absolute, since it is creative. This presence of the pleroma justifies the attribution to Christ of a cosmic role. For if the fullness is in him, any participation can depend only on him. The priority over all things—'he is before all things'—which creates so strange a problem for our way of thinking, is a logical consequence of the presence of the pleroma in Christ: the fullness always comes first, preceding all participation.

[1] The expression 'in Christ', 'in him', for the apostle always means for the apostle the Christ of glory.

If theologians thought they had to deny Christ a cosmic role, it was because they ignored the incomparable glory which scripture perceives in Christ in his resurrection. This participation in creation is an indubitably divine prerogative; but in his glorification Christ is wholly and entirely divine.[1] What is incomprehensible is not primarily this creative role, but this pleroma of the risen Christ, the conferring of the 'Name' which is nothing other than the lordship of God granted to Christ and which is exercised on the existence of things. There lies the unfathomable mystery: in the incarnation of God, in Christ's total union with God. The rest, the creative role, is the result of this. Raised to the pinnacle of all things, to the heights of God, Christ necessarily descends to the ultimate origin of things, which are all made for him (Eph 4:9ff.).

The beloved Son is the eschatological Christ

But of all this lordship, so strikingly asserted, we can say —not without regret—with the author of the Epistle to the Hebrews (2:8): 'As it is, we do not yet see everything in subjection to him.' In the epistles to the Colossians and Ephesians the apostle's vision becomes prophetic: it grasps the world's realities in their source, in the Christ of glory, in whom God at one stroke realized all the ultimate perfection of the world and completed the whole cosmic revolution, when he made dwell in him that fullness outside which nothing exists.

[1] The glorification is the fullness of the mystery of the incarnation, where the humanity of Christ is wholly assumed in God. The Fathers often speak of a total divinisation of Christ in his resurrection. Cf below, p. 54.

The subjection of the universe to Christ is not completed in the course of history, nor are all things reconciled in him. How many cracks there are in the world, how many scattered fragments! The world is created for Christ, but has not yet reached his level. The great epistles—more sensitive than those of the captivity to the slow processes of history—promise universal submission and pacification only for the last day (1 Cor 15:24-28). But they are already present in their source, the final reality is already accomplished in Christ, the eschatological resurrection is total in him who henceforward is the perfect image of God.[1] Facing him is a world as yet only in partial union with the fullness.

The dominion of Christ is both eschatological and paschal. His glorification has made him master of the last day, 'the last Adam,' 'the heavenly man' who comes at the end and who must renew the world (1 Cor 15:45-49). His precedence therefore is not related to the duration of the world; he entered late into history; in his glorification he is even the last, the term of a history of which he is the origin. He is first in as much as he is last, the transcendent fullness in which all things begin and end, the Alpha and the Omega (Rev 1:17; 22:13).[2]

II—THE CONNECTIONS BETWEEN CREATION AND REDEMPTION

In the light of this great scripture text, we must now try to define the mutual connections between the first creation of man and his salvation realized in Christ.

---

[1] 'This title of image of God is here presented as a characteristic of the eschatological Saviour.' A. Feuillet, op. cit., 169.
[2] Cf Church in the Modern World, 45.

The creation of the world begins with its term

If Christ is at the origin of everything because he is its ultimate fullness, the basis and centre of humanity must be in its zenith that is to come; things and the sequence of time must be dependent on their term, in which they find fulfilment and unity; nothing will make sense or be completely intelligible except in this final realization. Any christian reflection on man and his destiny therefore must be first of all eschatological, must try to find in the light of the end the explanation of the beginning and of the whole:[1] this is the trend of the apostle's thought, starting from the final redemption in order to go back to the origin.[2]

If we want to understand the mystery of the creative act, we must see it as a creative call, as an effective attraction to ultimate fullness. As St John puts it, Christ's dominion will be imposed by attraction: 'When I am lifted up from the earth—on the cross and in glory,

[1] *Church in the Modern World*, 10, 2: 'The Church believes that in her most benign Lord and Master can be found the key, the focal point, and the goal of all human history.'
[2] In the Old Testament already the work of creation is understood in the light of the experience of a God who saves his people, cf. E. Jacob, *Theology of the Old Testament*, London 1958, 148. It could be said that the theology of the redemption is prior to that of creation, cf. G. W. H. Lampe, 'La doctrine néotestamentaire de la création' in *Verbum Caro*, 73 (1965), 16.
The vocabulary used in Colossians to describe Christ's cosmic role had served in the previous epistles to express his role in the redemption. The formula, 'in him' everything subsists, recalls 'the source of your life in Christ Jesus' (1 Cor 1:30); 'the first-born of all creation' could in fact be derived from 'the first-born from the dead' and 'the first fruits of those who have fallen asleep'. Cf A. Feuillet, *op. cit.*, 269f.

where Christ exercises his divine prerogatives (Jn 8:28) —I will draw all men (or everything) to myself' (12:32).

This is why earthly things—which scripture calls 'carnal'—historically precede the true realities, those which do not fail, which are called 'spiritual': 'It is not the spiritual which is first but the physical, and then the spiritual' (1 Cor 15:46). The history of salvation proceeds from the flesh to the spirit, from man created as 'a living being' (1 Cor 15:45)—therefore not in a fullness of humanity and of grace—it proceeds towards the Christ of glory who is 'the Spirit' (2 Cor 3:17), reality in its divine fullness. This again is why the 'carnal' realities announce the necessary advent of the realities of the spirit: 'If there is a physical body, there is (then) also a spiritual body' (1 Cor 15:44);[1] for the imperfect realities exist in virtue of a fullness that is to come. As the apostle sees them, all the realities of the Old Testament are the shadow cast before, going back to the origins of the world, of a body to come: 'These are only a shadow of what is to come; but the substance (which casts this shadow) belongs to Christ' (Col 2:17). If the shadow exists, the body that casts it exists also and its existence is more real (cf also Eph 5:32). This is why finally the human race is *one*, radically one. Beginning with a first man in the past, mankind could only go on dispersing indefinitely, but in the Christ to come it finds not only its source, but the universal point of its convergence.

It seems then that a christian theology which takes up

[1] It seems in fact that, for the apostle, Adam is 'a type of the one who *had to* come' (cf Rom 5:14), that the baptism prefigured in Moses demands the existence of the true baptism, that manna exists because of the eucharist. Cf G. Martelet, 'Sacraments, figures et exhortation en 1 Cor X, 1-11' in *Rech. Sc. Rel.* 44 (1956), 523-31.

again the thought of the Old Testament in the light of Christ cannot place paradise and original justice solely at the first entry of mankind into history. For the ancient mentality which attributed power over the world to God alone, creation had to emerge finished and perfect from the hands of the creator. Man in the past therefore tended to place at the origin of things that which he made the object of his aspirations: man's complete rectitude, paradisial happiness, the golden age of humanity. Modern man cannot accept perspectives like these, since he thinks he knows through the sciences of pre-history the original precariousness of the human condition, believes in evolution and wants to contribute to the construction of the world. The christian too, trying to understand the history of the world through faith in the incarnation and in the light of such texts as Colossians 1:15–20, finds it scarcely possible to place paradisial perfection at the origins of mankind. St Paul set himself the task of giving a christian meaning to the Old Testament (2 Cor 3:15–17): he knew that the second Adam 'became a life-giving spirit', while the first had been created only as 'a living being' (1 Cor 15:45); that perfection belongs not to the beginning, but to the term. Man will therefore find paradise at the end, at the point where creation is completed,[1] 'in the heavenly places (that is) in Christ Jesus' (Eph 2:6); there too is found original justice, that of Christ, towards which he must climb.

Nevertheless, this justice is original also in time: the history of men begins in paradise. For, from the beginning, man was created for the fullness which is in

[1] According to the New Testament, God continues to create. Cf Jn 5:17.

Christ, for a total communion with God: he is created therefore in an original justice and from that time onwards an inhabitant of the future paradise where he is a son of God.

Creation is a filial reality

'In him all things were created', in Christ's power as Lord, in his radiant glory as image of God. But this power and this glory are proper to him as the beloved Son, as begotten by the Father. The glorification of Jesus is nothing other than the mystery of sonship in its full realisation: 'This he has fulfilled in raising Jesus, as it is written, "Thou art my Son, today I have begotten thee" ' (Acts 13:33). His power is that of his sonship: 'Son of God in power by his resurrection' (Rom 1:4). It is in begetting Christ that God gives him this role in the world, that he acts in him on the world, for 'whatever the Father gives the Son, he gives by begetting him.'[1]

The creation of the world thus prolongs the mystery of the incarnation. God creates when he begets his Son, Christ: he creates from this generation onwards, beginning with the image of himself that is Christ, a divine begetting which is simultaneously the dawn of creation. In his humanity Christ is the primordial creature of a world which—beginning with him—becomes in a sense wholly and entirely filial. It is therefore possible for man to find God within this world—the sapiential books and St Paul say so—to find him, not only with the aid of laborious reasoning, but in contemplating the world, its beauty, its grandeur, in this 'smile of God through the world', the radiance of the mystery of the incarnation.

[1] St Augustine, *Tract. in Joh.*, 106, 7, *CCL* 36, 613.

Of man above all, and of every man, it can be said that he leads—up to a point—a filial life, on condition that he lives in conformity with God's creative plan:[1] *immortal* son of God, because he lives by the Son of God raised up forever; immortal therefore in himself, since he is created in the risen Christ and for him, and again immortal by the resurrection of Christ.

To the extent to which creation is filial, not perverted by sin, it is also God's word, the expression of his being, of his plan and of what he wills. It is the fullness itself of the word in him who is at its culmination and at its origin. It is therefore essential for the church to know this world with its aspirations and its longings which are a language of God.[2] We must consider the world, inasmuch as it is human, with the utmost goodwill: for it is a prophecy and the remote preparation for the grace with which it is itself laden.

A world created within the redemption

If God creates us in the Christ of glory, we must conclude that he has only one plan[3] both creative and redemptive: it must mean that God creates man within the mystery of the redemption. For, as revealed in

[1] *Church in the Modern World*, 3, 2: 'A godlike seed has been sown in man'.
[2] *Church in the Modern World*, 4, 1: 39, 3.
[3] The unity of the work of creation is presupposed in several other texts of scripture. According to Ephesians 1:10, God's plan is both cosmic and soteriological. On Hebrews 2:10, 'it was fitting that he, for whom and by whom all things exist, in bringing many sons to glory, should make the pioneer of their salvation perfect through suffering', C. Spicq comments that to be destined to glory is inseparable from creation, 'bringing to glory' is merely an application of 'by whom all things exist'. *L'Epître aux Hébreux*, II, Paris 1953, 37.

scripture, Christ is essentially the saviour, Son of God for the salvation of men, 'raised up for us' in his redemptive death. It is in his glory as Saviour that he is the image of God in which all is created and the pleroma in which everything subsists.

In some way therefore man is christian at the level of his creation: his opening to God's creative action is already at least an initial opening to Christ and to final salvation; every authentic human value bears the imprint of the salvation which is in Christ, everything being created in Christ and for him.[1] *Anima naturaliter christiana.*[2] To be created is to be called to Christ. Once again therefore man is already saved in some way at the level of his human existence, being created in the Christ of glory, salvation of the world. The universal salvific will of God is written into human reality. God is (in all senses) the supreme realist, his plan of salvation is a will that becomes reality.

For man to fail to be saved therefore, he would have to get

---

[1] Cf *Church in the Modern World*, 38, 1; 39, 2, 3; 45, 2, 3.
[2] Tertullian, *Apol.*, 17, 6. *CCL* 1, 117. 'There is no nation which is not christian', *Ad nat.*, I, 8, 9. *CCL* 1, 22. But cf below, p. 42, n.1.

In this perspective, the relations between nature and grace may be understood in this way: in the concrete, there is no such thing as a state of pure nature, man is created for his supernatural end. 'Nature' is man as he can be conceived when we abstract from the attraction exercised by God to draw him to this end. It is Christ who is the supernatural element in the world, Son of God in the Holy Spirit; the supernatural element is also the attraction exercised by God, drawing man to Christ. Of himself man cannot be saved, it is by creation for the fullness that he will be saved. Of himself he has no right to salvation: to be created is something to which he has no right and the more elevated is the creative action, so much the greater is its gratuitousness.

out of this plan, he would have to get out of it by refusing the salvation for which he is created.

Certainly men must use the means ordained for salvation. Nevertheless, they will not fail to be saved if these means are lacking, but only if they refuse them. God has revealed what man must do to be saved: he must give his faith. But God has not revealed what he will do himself for those who die before they possess the ordinary means of reaching faith. Even before they are able to seek God, men are sought by him in Christ: they will not fail to be saved unless they leave the order of salvation— that is to say, through their own fault.[1]

It is true that mankind became sinful from the beginning and that each man belongs from birth to this sinful humanity. But sin *super*vened, came on top; it affects man at the second stage of his existence, in his belonging to other men. It affects him very deeply, in his very nature, for he would not be truly man apart from this belonging to other men. And yet man belongs to the second Adam, his saviour, more radically than to the first. Before he is a member of a sinful community, he is created by God and for Christ. It can even be said that forgiveness of sins comes first, it is sufficient for man unceasingly to accept this.[2]

[1] According to *Church in the Modern World*, 22, 2, 'by his incarnation the Son of God has united himself in some fashion with every man.'
[2] On the question of original sin we may be permitted to raise the following points:
Original sin does not involve any personal culpability. This is admitted, in theory at least, by all theologians (cf DS 1006). It is the sin of the human community, become sinful from the dawn of its history. It does however affect the individual human being profoundly, since belonging to other men is an essential dimension of human personality.

Since everything is created in the saving lordship of Christ, earthly realities too *can* be bearers of salvation for us;[1] all events *can* be referred to the great event, the death and resurrection of Christ.[2] Even before they know Christ, men help one another on the way of salvation, if they help one another to be truly human. In order to understand better the truths of salvation revealed to her, the church must also listen to the world in which the leaven of salvation is already at work.

What is more, human beings on earth are all in some way members of the church,[3] to the extent that they

---

This sin is overcome in baptism (DS 1514), where man comes to share in eschatological justice such as it is in Christ and enters into fellowship with a humanity marked not by sin, but by sanctity: the communion of saints.

According to the essential scripture text that dominates the theology of original sin, Rom 5:12, it does not seem that 'the sin of nature' involves of itself eternal death, that of itself it excludes salvation. Man is excluded from salvation by personal sin to which, without the grace of Christ, every human being would succumb under the burden of the 'sin of nature': 'As sin (the dominion of sin) came into the world through one man and death (eternal death, expressed and realised in physical death) through sin, and so death (this eternal death) spread to all men (abstracting from the saving grace of Christ) because all men sinned.' This at any rate is the interpretation generally accepted by exegetes. Every human being without fail acquiesces in the dominion of sin in the world and thus incurs condemnation (apart from redemptive grace).

[1] Cf *Bishops*, 12: 'Earthly goods are also related to man's salvation and can contribute much to the upbuilding of Christ's body.'

[2] *Church in the Modern World*, 38: Christ 'entered the world's history, taking that history up into himself and summarizing it.'

[3] *Church*, 13: 'All men are called to be part of this catholic unity of the People of God, belong to it or are related to it

accept the creative plan of God. They belong to the church by their roots, these roots of their being by which they live already on their future, Christ, for whom they are created.

For the church, in the world, is the sacrament of the presence and action of Christ by which the world is and must become filial. Having realized the pleroma in Christ, God fills up the church with this fullness (Col 2:9) to the point at which it becomes in its turn the pleroma, the very body of Christ (Col 1:18); Eph 1:23), the sacrament for men of their creation in Christ: '(God) has made (Christ) the head over all things for the church, which is his body, the fullness of him (Christ) who fills all in all.'

In her mystery the church is the culmination of humanity within the world, a culmination not yet attained by the rest of the world, but already immanent in it by the action of God who creates humanity for the redeeming Christ. The church is not apart because of her election; she is built at the heart of the city of men. Among men she constitutes the narrowest circle in which Christ is present to all mankind and acts upon it. From this fullness outwards the grace of God seeks to spread to all men. The church is not only the symbol of the world's salvation, but also the leaven in the whole (Mt 13:33),[1] the leaven which must gradually penetrate everywhere; this she is by her testimony and teaching and first of all by her presence at the heart of mankind with Christ whose body she is. The communion of saints spreads its

in various ways.' This orientation does not exist merely in God's plan, for the latter is always at least beginning to be realized.

[1] *Church in the Modern World*, 40, 2.

light beyond the church of faith and the sacraments, as
the action of Christ itself, towards all men right back to
the origins of history,[1] towards all men around it in
space, who do not knowingly and effectively cut themselves off from it. The axiom 'Outside the church no
salvation' means, when it is positively formulated, that
the church and she alone in the world is the source of
salvation for all men of good will. When therefore christians go out to meet other human beings in order to
bring them the message of Christ and of the church, the
grace of Christ *and* of the church will have preceded
them.[2] God's initiative in Christ and in the church is
absolute: it does not come to help man to enter into the
order of salvation, it creates him within that order and
directs him to salvation by way of the human reality itself. The apostle who brings the message must therefore
be attentive to the road already travelled by men, to
the ecclesial values they already possess; he must respect

[1] H. de Lubac, *Méditation sur l'Eglise*, Paris 1953, 48: 'What
is true of him (first-born of all creation) is true also of the
church, his spouse. Prepared like him for long ages by the
history of the Jewish people, prefigured in the earthly paradise, she is, like him, in reality more ancient still. She must
be seen in God, before the beginning of the world . . .
Hermas was not wrong therefore when he saw her in a
vision under the guise of an old woman; for, as his guide, the
shepherd, explained, she was created first, before everything,
that is to say, the world was made for her.' Cf Hermas, *The
Shepherd*, 2, 4. See other quotations from the Fathers in de
Lubac, *loc. cit.*
[2] The grace of Christ, which reaches human beings before
they are touched by the church's ministry, is also ecclesial
grace. The church is with Christ at the heart of the world,
for the salvation of the world: she is active, not only as
visible sacrament, but also by her profound mystery; by her
charity, her prayer and her suffering, she can help those
remote from her whom her word will never reach.

their aspirations, the riches of civilisation of a people and its religious feeling.[1] To act otherwise would be to compromise the dynamism of the grace which has always been at work in these men's hearts directing them towards faith.

This salvation is still to be realized

Basically, men have received baptism: they are in some way christian, in some way saved. Nevertheless, the church would be wrong to say to herself: 'Why impose on me the heavy burden of an uncertain apostolate? They are christians, they are saved! Why provoke a crisis, making them face a decision for or against Christ and the church, since they are already christians even without this decision? Isn't it sufficient to help them fraternally to be human beings, simply human beings?'

From all the evidence of scripture, salvation is not immanent in such a way that man needs only to exist and develop horizontally—so to speak—on the level at which he began to be. Salvation is at the centre of mankind, but on another level and prior to man: an inner peak which remains to be climbed. Mankind must surpass itself in order to advance towards what it is in Christ. He in whom and for whom everything *is created is the eschatological Christ*: he draws men from the height of the cross and we reach him by rising above our first state, in an 'elevation above the earth'.[2] *'People are not*

---

[1] Cf *Church*, 13; *Missions*, 9 and 22.
[2] I am not saying that man is saved by going beyond himself, but by going beyond his first state; heaven is not separated from earthly life, but is the interiorisation and fulfilment of this. But this fulfilment is possible only by the creative intervention of God.

born, but become Christians.'[1] The reality of salvation consists in this final reality which is Christ dead and risen: in human values it exists as yet only in the form of a more or less distant promise. Salvation is an objective to which man is called.

God creates by a call, by his creating and attracting Word, Christ dead and risen, who is salvation. Man is not already saved in what he is, but in what he becomes in Christ. If God were to refuse to bring about this becoming beyond his first state, man would not be saved. If man were to resist the process of becoming, he would cut himself off from salvation. We have said that, to fail to be saved, man would have to get out of the plan of salvation: he gets out of it when he renounces the fullness for which he never ceases to be created.

Earthly things are in some way Christian, as related to this ultimate fullness. Ambivalent in themselves, they must be surpassed in the use that is made of them. They are like the shadow cast by a body. It is possible to be attached to these things without regard to their ultimate fullness and then the shadow is taken for the reality, there is a refusal of the process of becoming, a lapse into idolatry.[2] Man must therefore renounce himself un-

[1] The words are Tertullian's (*Apol.* 18,4,*CCL*, 1, 118), although he also speaks of an *anima naturaliter christiana*. Elsewhere, he also says: 'You are not, as far as I know, a christian: for you become, you are not born, a christian.' *De testim. animae* 17, *CCL* 1, 176. When he speaks of a soul that is naturally christian, Tertullian is not saying that a pagan is already a christian, but that he has within him dispositions which accord with Christianity and testify in his favour. Cf N. Brox, 'Anima naturaliter christiana' in *Zeitschrift für katholische Theologie* 91 (1969), 70–5.

[2] 'All human activity must be purified and perfected by the power of Christ's cross and resurrection.' *Church in the Modern World*, 37.

ceasingly, undertake continually to surpass himself; he
must consent to his progressive creation towards fullness.
It is this going beyond oneself for the sake of fullness that
scripture calls dying to 'the flesh'.

This dying—a total death—is written into the very term of
human becoming, in Christ who is its ultimate fullness, glorified
in a permanent death to 'the flesh'.

And this term is a *redemptive* death, proof for man of his
essential need to be saved from sin. So far as he fails to
share in this glorifying death, he is a sinner: he is so by
the margin of shadow that encircles his earthly existence, for anyone who lacks the glorious holiness of God
is a sinner (Rom 3-23); he is so even more through the
sin in which the whole human community is implicated
from the beginning and through his personal sins.[1]
Created for a Christ glorified in death, man has a deep-
rooted need to die to himself; death is part of the mystery of creation.[2] But, as willed by God, it is a pasch, a
passing, a consent to fullness.

The church's necessary apostolate

The eschatological fullness is offered for man's consent in
as much as Christ enters into the world and encounters

[1] Scripture permits us to distinguish three different levels in
sin: personal sin, the sin that rules over the totality of mankind (Rom 5:12) and finally the imperfect state of man on
earth. Christ himself was involved in this state because of the
fact of his earthly 'flesh' (Rom 8:3; 2 Cor 5:21); he surpasses
it in his 'death to sin' (Rom 6:10) and his 'justification' in
the glory of the Spirit (1 Tim 3:16).
[2] Scripture does not teach that, without Adam's sin, man
would have been immortal on earth, that he would not have
been subject to this law of wholly surpassing himself. The
death of which Rom 5:12 speaks, the consequence of sin, is
the end of life in estrangement from God, a condemnation of
man for ever.

men. He does this in the church and through his apostolate. Since any authentic human value depends on the
grace of Christ, the conclusion is sometimes drawn that
every truly human being is truly a christian, a christian
who most often is unaware of the fact and to whom the
church has the mission of revealing his christian identity:
she must place him in the presence of Christ in whom he
will recognise himself. The mission of the church, in this
view, is not to bring grace, but to make people aware of
its presence.

This however is not her essential mission. It is useful
for man to come to know what he is already; but what is
really important is to bring into being what does not yet
exist. If the church had no other role than that of making men aware of a salvation already realised, she would
not be necessary for salvation and the apostolate would
be of secondary importance, for it is more important to
be than to know. Although he has received much, man
has much still to receive: *he still has everything to receive*,
Christ, the totality of salvation.

Evangelisation is the 'epiphany' of the salvation to
come:[1] its revelation and its realisation. Through the
church, her life and her message, the eschatological
reality blazes a trail in the world, addresses its creative
call to men and is imparted to them. St Paul was conscious of a cosmic mission. He knew that he was endowed
with a force which is active in the glorification of Christ,
the creative force of the new world. Through the apostles
God pronounces the reconciling word (2 Cor 5:18–20),
by which he brings back everything under one head
(Eph 1:10): 'to reconcile to himself all things, whether
on earth or in heaven' (Col 1:20). Through the faith

[1] *Missions*, 9.

that the apostle rouses, through the sacraments he celebrates, man is incorporated into the body of Christ where the creation of men is begun and completed.

The duty of believing the apostle

It is not easy to believe in the mission of the church, in this power with which she is invested to perfect the creation of the world. Results which are often derisory, christians—that is, ourselves—who are so ineffective, our evident weakness: all these make our grandiose claims seem merely the fabric of a dream. But in christianity everything is paradoxical. There is a folly of the cross as well as faith in the cross (cf 1 Cor 1:18). Faith means sharing in the cross, and this is folly: faith is therefore folly.

Who will deny that this creative power of God is at work in the apostle if he believes that, in Christ and the church, men become 'a new creation' (2 Cor 5:17; Gal 6:15) and that the communion of saints is the new world? If we reflect on it, the very weakness of the church makes her faith and her hopes less incredible. Everything points to the fact that the only proportion between the creative power of God and man's action on earth is an apparently inverse ratio of greatness: that power is seen to be infinite only in weakness; that wisdom is revealed as divine only under the empty appearances of faith; and eternal life is visible in the death of Christ. Man is called to rule over creation, not only by subjecting it to himself (Gen 1:26), but by participating in the divine action on the world. This participation is most intense in the church, destined to lead the world to its final perfection; it is therefore normal for the church to resemble him who is the perfect image of God in his creative action: Christ in the mystery of his pasch.

3

REDEMPTION AND THE APOSTOLATE

Saint Paul is aware of being an apostle 'through Jesus
Christ and God the Father, who raised him from the
dead' (Gal 1:1); according to the synoptics, the apostles
are sent out with all that saving power with which
Christ was invested at his resurrection (Mt 28:18; Lk
24:49); according to the fourth gospel, they are consecrated and sent out in virtue of the pastoral consecration of Christ (Jn 17:18–19), that is to say, in virtue of
his glorifying death. The source of the apostolate lies
in the mystery of the redemption. We must therefore
look into this mystery if we are to appreciate properly
the church's apostolate.

There are however different theologies of the redemption. A theology is never more than one approach to the
mystery and some approach it only from a great distance, presenting a very uncertain image of the mystery
of redemption and—consequently—of the apostolate.

One of the main theories of the redemption, which
prevailed up to a short time ago, might be summed up
as follows:

Man has sinned. His offence is quasi-infinite, for the
person offended is infinite in majesty. No human being
can make adequate reparation for the infringement of
divine justice. Only a being whose merits were infinite
would be able to do this. The incarnation therefore was
necessary for the redemption. As Son of God, Christ
could have obtained forgiveness for us by any act at all

during his life on earth, since the least of these had infinite value. But, 'having loved his own to the end' and in order to underline both the rigours of divine justice and the enormity of the offence, he threw into the balance of merits and demerits—I say 'into the balance', for this theology used very juridical forms of expression—his suffering, his blood, his death. Thus sin is expiated, since the price has been paid: man is properly redeemed. Then, in a second, distinct and complementary act, God 'applies the merits of Christ', 'distributes' the benefits merited, particularly through the apostolic ministry: forgiveness, grace, eternal life.

In this perspective, the apostle does not collaborate directly with Christ in his redemptive work: his role is that of transmission and distribution. This mission does not involve a personal commitment, it can be discharged as a simple function. Christ himself had no need to become wholly involved, at the deeper levels of his being, since his role was limited to that of paying off a debt that was not his own. But if we start out from a system that completely ignores any saving role in the resurrection of Christ, is it possible to grasp the real meaning of an apostolate which, according to scripture, derives its force, not only from the death of Christ, but first and foremost from his resurrection?

Of its nature, Western thought has always been inclined to exploit the juridical aspect of the redemption in the light of some of the scriptural images: ransom (Mt 20:28), repurchase at a high price (1 Cor 6:20; 7:23)—the word 'redemption' itself means 'buying back'. But this theological exploitation of juridical terminology confers an absolute value on what is meant to be merely an analogy, an illustration of a greater truth in terms of human realities. This language anyway had lost much of its primitive meaning and, far from finding support in scripture, juridical theology comes up against more serious objections.

First and foremost, *to whom must the ransom be paid*? The early writers replied: to the devil, for it was from slavery to him that men had to be ransomed. This was an odd kind of theology and was soon abandoned. But was the answer subsequently given any better? This was to the effect that the price had to be paid to God, to appease his justice and anger and to win his favour. This meant that man, in Jesus Christ, took the initiative and won God's favour for men. And yet 'God is love', a father who is always waiting for his prodigal son, a shepherd who looks for his lost sheep, a God who from all eternity has at heart the plan of salvation (Eph 1:4–11): 'God so loved the world that he gave his only Son, that whoever believes in him should not perish but have eternal life' (Jn 3:16; cf 6:38–40). It is not God who has to be reconciled with us, but we 'who are reconciled with him who loves us and with whom we were at enmity through sin.'[1] St Paul had said: 'while we were enemies we were reconciled to God' (Rom 5:10; 2 Cor 5:18–20). It is God who redeems us (Rev 14:3): he redeems us, not as objects, but in the way that men are won over, offering them his friendship, making them enter into fellowship with him.

The juridical theory compels us to raise further questions. If Christ is dead, the ransom is paid, *the matter is*

[1] St Augustine, *In Johannem, tract.* 110, 6, *CCL* 36, 626. 'In Him (Christ) God reconciled us to Himself and among ourselves' (*Church in the Modern World*, 22, 3). The Second Vatican Council always expresses itself in this way (cf *Church in the Modern World*, 78, 3; *Missions*, 3).

settled once and for all and belongs to the past: henceforth God distributes the benefits won by Christ. Why then is a church necessary? why are the sacraments indispensable? and the effort to live a christian life that cannot be avoided if we are to be saved? Isn't it sufficient to believe that Christ has paid off the debt? From this standpoint, faith alone is necessary, a faith that consists in believing that Christ has paid in my place and in availing myself of his merits. Finally, why Christ's resurrection? If everything has been settled by his death, nothing further is needed.[1]

St Paul however writes: 'If Christ has not been raised, . . . you are still in your sins' (1 Cor 15:17). If the apostle is telling the truth, if sin is not destroyed unless Christ is risen, an appreciation of the death of Christ in which the resurrection plays a merely supererogatory role, where death suffices without reference to glory, if not erroneous, is at least incomplete. It is in fact so seriously incomplete that, when the theologians of the Reformation drew the logical conclusions, they fell into errors in faith.

Another consequence of the juridical theory is this: if the redemption is explained in terms only of the death, without reference to the glory, then *the significance of this death itself is obscured, its very necessity denied*. For, in the light of this sytem, it can be said that any action at all of Christ would have sufficed for men's redemption; that the death in itself was useless. If Christ died, it was the result of a superabundant love and a way of giving an example of a wonderful patience.

[1] Although the theory is superseded, this system survives in the numerous misunderstandings it has created. As a result of thinking that the death alone has saving power, some have been led to believe that Christ's glorification can be relegated to the realm of myth without prejudice to faith.

All this seems to contradict the clear assertions of Scripture: 'The Son of man must be killed' (Mk 8:31); 'The Son of man must be lifted up' (Jn 3:14); 'Was it not necessary that Christ should suffer these things?' (Lk 24:26), for 'without the shedding of blood there is no forgiveness of sins' (Heb 9:22).

Faced by this scriptural evidence, juridical theology attributes the redemption to the death of Christ; nevertheless, when we look more closely, the redemption is not attributed to the death itself, but to the sufferings, the patience and the merits which preceded it. Yet, according to scripture, the death of Christ is itself redemptive: it is this which transforms and changes into life the death in which man is cursed; it is in death that Christ wins the glory which is the salvation of the world. The earthly actions of Christ also contribute to the redemption, but in their outcome—which is death (cf Phil 2:7-9). Summing up in a word the whole earthly life of Christ, the apostle says: 'he died for all' (1 Cor 15:3; 2 Cor 5:15).

A final question: is a purely juridical theology *faithful to Old Testament prophecy*? Through the prefigurings of the redemption which God multiplied for Israel's sake, delivering that people over and over again from the hands of its enemies, it is in this rhythm of death and resurrection that salvation is achieved. In the numerous psalms in which the New Testament caught an anticipated echo of the voice of the suffering and triumphant Christ, it is not death which is salvation: death is an evil from which the psalmist asks to be delivered, salvation is a gift of life similar to a resurrection.

The prophets of the exile announced the redemption as a deliverance, as the return to Yahweh's land, the resurrection of a people whose bones were scattered in the valley (Ezek 37); as God's presence among his own and a marvellous outpouring of the Spirit of holiness. Israel will be saved when it can be said, 'God is with us' (Is 7:14; 8:10), and when Jersualem is called 'the City of the Lord, the Zion of the Holy One of Israel' (Is 60: 14). *Salvation will be fellowship with God.*

In the biblical perspective, the unredeemed world is a world cut off from God, deprived of his holiness—'all have sinned and fall short of the glory of God' (Rom 3:23)—closed in on an autonomy of misery. Cut off from the holiness which alone renders man just and which is at the same time the power of eternal life, man is both sinner and doomed to death. He may well appear to be alive, but in reality he is not merely mortal—he is dead: 'your bodies are dead because of sin' (Rom 8:10).

The evil afflicting unredeemed man is solitude, being outside God's fellowship. Scripture calls man in this state 'carnal': 'While we were living in the flesh . . .' (Rom 7:5). And it is the flesh that is opposed to the Spirit (Gal 5:17). The latter is holiness, life and divine power, and at the same time charity and the gift of self. Flesh refers to man in sin, in the mortal weakness and egoism of his closed existence. Twice St Paul uses the image of a prison (Gal 3:22; Rom 11:32), in which sinful man is confined: 'Who will deliver me from this body of death?' (Rom 7:24).

In order to rescue men from their damnation, is it sufficient for Christ to pay the price of forgiveness, dying in their place? How could someone save them by dying in their place? In wartime another person may offer to die for a hostage. In this sense, one man can die for another. But no one can do this for a person whose death is written into his existence; you don't save a dying man by being shot in his place. Redemption is a creation for a fullness of life of which man is incapable, against which he even closes himself up by sin. God saves men when he draws them out of their condition of 'flesh', *bringing them into a communion of life with him.*[1]

I—SALVATION REALISED IN CHRIST

God gives himself to men in Jesus Christ. The incarnation is the mystery of union and, for that reason, mystery of salvation. It opens—and salvation with it—in the advent on earth of the Son of God; through death it reaches its glorious fullness and thus in Christ the work of redemption is accomplished.

Christ in the 'flesh'

During Christ's earthly life his union with his Father was not complete in every respect: the Son of God had taken on the human condition in the form that scripture calls an existence according to the flesh (Rom 8:3). And it is characteristic of the flesh to be closed up, deprived of the Spirit: an existence that is not animated by the life-giving glory of God (Jn 17:5), doomed to solitude (Jn 12:24), restricted in its activity, subject to death. Christ found himself in his earthly existence integrated into this world, which is closed up in itself and in need of salvation: 'Who, though he was in the form of God, did not count equality with God a thing to be grasped, but emptied himself, taking the form of a servant, being

[1] *Church*, 7: 'The Son of God redeemed man and transformed him into a new creation by overcoming death through his own death and resurrection.' Vatican II normally thinks in terms of communion, participation, fellowship. Cf, e.g., *Church*, 2; *Revelation*, 2; *Missions*, 2.

born in the likeness of men. And being found in human
form he humbled himself' (Phil 2:6-8).

He was the Son of God and yet remote from his Father whom he had still to rejoin. He was in the bosom of
this Father and yet so imperfectly possessed by his life-
giving glory that he could succumb to death. The incarnation is a mystery of total union, in which God imparts himself wholly to a man, in which this man makes
only one with God; at this time the mystery had not yet
had its full effect in Christ.

*The drama of redemption had to be played out wholly and
entirely in Christ himself.* The salvation he had to gain for
us, he had to obtain first for himself. The Epistle to the
Hebrews recalls a prayer offered by Christ in the flesh, a
prayer of deep distress addressed to his God and Father,
to be saved from death: 'In the days of his flesh, Jesus
offered up prayers and supplications, with loud cries and
tears, to him who was able to save him from death' (Heb
5:7). He did not ask to be exempted from death, for—
it is said—he was heard (5:7) and yet he suffered death.
He asked to be saved in the glory of his Father (cf. 5:9);
he aspired to the total union with his Father in which
lies the salvation of man: 'Glorify thou me *in thy own
presence* with the glory which I had with thee' (Jn 17:5;
13:32).

The redemption therefore was a personal sanctification:[1] 'For their sake I consecrate myself' (Jn 17:19).
This word must be taken in its biblical sense of a setting
apart for God, a passing from the profane state into

---

[1] This personal character of the redemptive action will be
found again in the whole christian reality. We shall see that
there is no apostolic activity which is purely external to the
person of the apostle.

God's holiness. It is true that Christ was already holy, with the holiness of the Son of God, and yet he says: 'I consecrate myself.' Between himself and the Father there was a distance to be covered—of which he says, 'I am going to the Father'—not a spatial distance, but the distance between life according to the flesh and life in the bosom of the Father. He covered it by sanctifying himself. He renounces his existence according to the flesh— which is in a sense profane, because closed up in itself— and submits to the life-giving holiness of God flooding in upon him.

The redemption cannot be reduced to payment of a debt: it involves the person of Christ. For him, more intensely than any man, death is an existential event, the 'Hour' of his filial destiny, the passing from this world to the Father (Jn 13:1). In death Jesus is 'lifted up from the earth' to the presence of God (Jn 12:32; Rev 12:5); it is there that he is in all truth the beloved Son of God (Jn 10:17). The redemption is a filial mystery, *it is the total divinisation of the man Jesus, his entry into full union with his Father*. The incarnation, this mystery of 'the Word made flesh, whose glory we have seen' (Jn 1:14), 'of him whom the Father consecrated' (Jn 10:36) and 'who is in the bosom of the Father' (Jn 1:18), making only one with him (Jn 10: 30): the incarnation reaches its supreme truth in the glorifying death.

Henceforward God's saving will, this will to bring man into union with God, is realised to infinity in Christ. One man, Jesus Christ, is within the mystery of God, totally begotten by God (Acts 13:33), heir to God's own name (Phil 2:9), filled with the divine fullness (Col 1:19). God gives him life in the Holy Spirit and makes him the source of the Spirit for all men (1 Cor 15:45).

The salvific meaning of Christ's death

Death cannot therefore be understood without reference to glory, its redemptive significance can lie only in
this reference: 'I lay down my life, that I may take it
again' (Jn 10:17), says Christ; 'I die in order to rise',
explains St Augustine,[1] to rise to a new and ever new
existence, for 'the death he died he died to sin, once
for all, but the life he lives he lives to God' (Rom
6:10).

Death is the part of the man Jesus in this divinising
union: the man consents to the will of God which has
the power to save man; he receives it, delivers himself
up to this life-giving will. Consequently we see why
death was necessary, for it is only in death that man can
commit himself completely, in a fullness of receptive submission. We see that this death, if it is also to have its
full saving power, must be that of the Son of God, for
the Son alone can go to his Father; in him alone God
can realize this total communion; in him alone the reception could be vast enough to receive in its whole extent the infinity of divine holiness, this pleroma, thanks
to which Christ is placed at the summit and at the origin
of all in order to realize the salvation of all. The earthly
life too was redemptive because—according to St
John's thought, prepared to some extent in St Luke—
it was already paschal, wholly oriented to his death and
glory. As for the sufferings of the passion, they are redemptive because of the obedience unto death that they
prepare: 'Although he was a Son, he learned obedience
through what he suffered and was made perfect' (Heb
5:8-9). For the man who loves, the ordeal of suffering is

[1] *In Johannem, tract.* 47, 7, *CCL,* 36, 407.

undoubtedly the best key for opening to God the deepest recesses of his feeling.

It is in this way that the death of Christ is a sacrifice in the sense of St Augustine's very appropriate definition: 'a work by which man dies to the world in order to live to God' and 'to adhere to him in a holy society.'[1] It is the sacrifice *par excellence*, for the communion of the man Jesus with his Father is total. In his glorifying death, Christ is the culmination of the work of creation, for God creates by imparting himself and in order to impart himself.

It is appropriate therefore to purify or rather to deepen a number of theological notions. Redemption is not a gift offered to God to appease his justice: *it is the total gift of God to the man Jesus and the Jesus' total acceptance of this gift*. It is true that Christ's sacrifice is an 'offering' (Eph 5:2), but it is an oblation of himself whereby man receives in himself the God whom he loves and his saving creative dominion. Then God in his turn is totally delivered up to man in the gift he makes of himself and in the acceptance that he gives to his creature: the redemption is a mystery of love.

Redemptive *merit* cannot be understood according to the law of *do ut des*, of barter, in which Christ would give his blood in return for forgiveness and grace, but as the moral and physical disposition for receiving the infinite gift of God.[2] Christ consented with a total acquiescence to the will of his Father (Heb 10:5-7) and 'therefore' he was exalted (Phil 2:9). To merit means actively to consent to receive God's holiness offered to man. In his

[1] *De Civitate Dei* 10, 6, *CCL* 47, 278.
[2] St Thomas Aquinas, *De Veritate* q.29 a.7, defines merit as 'fitness for the reception of glory'.

obedience unto death, Christ receives the life-giving glory of the Father; the man who is Son of God merits God's sonship; in a supreme act of acceptance he enters into possession of the gift that the Father had made him from the beginning.

Merit such as this is personal, it cannot be 'distributed'. It must be recognised that the role of ministers of salvation, of apostles, cannot be that of distributing the merits of Christ. If there is a part allotted to them in the work of salvation, a work that is wholly personal to Christ, it will consist in a personal involvement in the mystery of Christ.

Expiation is not compensatory suffering. The gift of divine holiness and the acceptance of this gift alone can expiate sin. For sin means the refusal of divine justice, that is, of the life-giving holiness that God wants to impart: for what characterises the sinner is essentially his estrangement from God (cf Lk 15:14–20), his want of the glory of God (Rom 3:23). 'The sin of the world' is expiated in a communion with God: the Lamb of God expiates, deletes the sin of the world when in the fullness of his own 'sanctification' he becomes for men the source of the Holy Spirit (compare John 1:29–33 with 7:37–39; 19:34–36; 20:22–23).

The notion of *satisfaction*, created by theology, cannot be understood in a biblical context as restitution made to divine justice. It is by refusing to receive it that the life-giving and sanctifying justice of God, the justice by which God is just and which is the Holy Spirit, is infringed, in man's heart; Christ satisfies justice when he lets himself be 'vindicated in the Spirit' (1 Tim 3:16), when he lets himself fulfil justice to the point at which he becomes himself God's justice (1 Cor 1:30) and the source of justice for whoever believes in him (Rom 3:23–26; 4:25).

The eternal reality of redemption

Such an utterly complete salvation as that realised in Christ can only be eternal. Because death is the end of earthly life and because the risen Christ appeared to his disciples, his death and resurrection are written into history, but in themselves they are situated at the term of history and beyond it: they constitute an eschatological and eternal reality in which men are called to participate. The Epistle to the Hebrews says that Christ by his death reached 'the consummation': his death, by which he 'entered into heaven', is the final event, the ultimate reality of salvation.

God raises Christ by begetting him in his whole existence, human and divine: 'He has raised Jesus . . . as it is written, . . . "Thou art my Son, today I have begotten thee"' (Acts 13:33). This today of the divine generation is eternal and Christ never goes beyond the moment of his birth, he lives forever in the first instant of his filial newness, where he *is* wholly by his Father. for Christ then there is no more becoming beyond the 'pleroma' that is conferred on him (Col 1:9) or the Name which is bestowed on him (Phil 2:9): he lives in the instant of his glorification.

The death of Christ, too, is a final reality which will never be surpassed. For his death and resurrection are 'not so much two separate events as a mystery with two aspects'. Death and glorification coincide and glorification, being eternal, holds Christ forever in his redemptive death.

If we envisage the redeeming act in the light of the

different images with which scripture attempts to illustrate it, we always observe that death and glorification are simultaneous aspects of one and the same reality.

Thus scripture considers the death of Christ as a gift of himself, for a gift is made only at the moment when the other's acceptance corresponds to the gesture of the person offering it. And glorification is the Father's acceptance. Likewise scripture envisages the death as a sacrifice which is an entry into union with God. And the union is realized at the moment of Christ's meeting with the Father, at the moment of glorification. The death of Christ is a sacrifice in as much as it coincides with glory.

Scripture also considers Christ's death as a passing, a transformation, the end of the 'flesh' and the entry into existence according to the Spirit. In all transformation the end of one mode of being coincides with the beginning of another. And finally scripture considers the death as merit, to which glory corresponds. For to merit is to be disposed for the gift and to receive it. Death is the reception given to God's saving will, death and glorification are simultaneous.

Death therefore does not precede any more than glory follows. Since it is eternal, glorification maintains Christ forever in the reality of his death, at the moment of merit, in the reception given to the divine life, at the height of his self-giving. Redemption has not been merely gained, *it remains an event for ever*: Christ is not only Saviour, he is salvation, redemption achieved.

The mystery of the incarnation, mystery of infinite communion of man and God, is also the eschatological mystery of the world, in which we are invited to take part: 'Being made perfect he became the source of eternal salvation to all who obey him' (Heb 5:9; cf Col 2:9).

II—CHRIST, MEDIATOR OF SALVATION

If Christ had died in place of men, it would be sufficient for God to distribute to them the forgiveness he had obtained. But the redemption was more than the payment of a debt, it was a personal sanctification, a drama played out entirely in Christ. Everything began in him, everything was achieved in him. The purpose of his death, the global object of his merit, was his resurrection. Christ's death did not sanctify anyone and will never sanctify anyone except Christ himself and those who are in him.

The extension to men of the redemption accomplished in Christ could not be realised by 'applying merits' in the strict sense of the formula. For the merits of Christ are not a thing; Christ merits for himself by the reception he gives in his death to the Father's glory: this merit is inalienably bound up with his person. Nor is it any more permissible to 'distribute' forgiveness and the grace won by Christ, since forgiveness and grace are no more a thing than is merit. Forgiveness and grace of sonship are God's action in begetting Christ, the glorious life of the Holy Spirit in which Christ is raised up. If there are ministries of this forgiveness and of this grace, then, once again, their part cannot consist in applying merits, in transmitting forgiveness and graces.

In order to describe the extension of the redemption to the world, scripture speaks in terms of communion.[1] Since salvation consists wholly in Christ, being personified in him (1 Cor 1:30) and in his glorifying death, men will benefit from it only by becoming a single body with

[1] So does Vatican II: man is 'linked with the paschal mystery' (*Church in the Modern World*, 22); he 'is sharing in the mystery of Christ's death and resurrection' (*Missions*, 13); he must 'live the paschal mystery' (*Priestly Formation*, 8).

him in his death and resurrection. That is why Christ tells them: 'Take, eat; this is my body given for you'.

Men take part in Christ's pasch (Lk 22:14–16; 22: 29–30); they eat the 'bread of life'. We do not distribute, we do not apply the nourishing power of bread: we distribute and we eat the bread itself. We do not merely appeal to the merits of Christ, we unite ourselves to Christ in his merit, that is, in his death. Men receive 'the sprinkled blood' (Heb 12:24; 1 Pet 1:2); they soak their soiled clothes in the blood of the Lamb (Rev 7:14); they are the shoots of the vine (Jn 15); they enter on the 'new and living way', which is nothing other than Christ in the reality of the redemptive mystery, and they have access with him to the presence of God, 'through the curtain, that is, through his flesh' which was immolated (Heb 10:20). They become christians through being integrated into Christ: 'He is the source of your life in Christ, . . . whom God made our . . . sanctification and redemption' (1 Cor 1:30). The Church is the very body of Christ.

This integration into Christ is effected as *a participation in the redemptive action,* since no one can be united with Christ except where he remains forever, as the Saviour and salvation of men: in his glorifying death. As he becomes one body with him, the christian dies to himself in the very death of Christ and rises by the same action of God who raises Christ (Rom 6:3–6; Gal 2:19; Eph 2:5–6; Col 2:12–13). He is saved to the extent to which he participates in 'the redemption which is in Christ' (Rom 3: 24).

The paschal Christ comes into this world

For the redemption to be extended to men, Christ himself therefore must come to them, must be offered to

them, and they must be able to enter into a fellowship
of salvation with him. Before dying, Christ announces
his coming. He does not say that he will return, but that
he is coming from now onwards, that he will appear to
men: 'From now on you will see the Son of man coming
. . . ' (Mt 26:64); 'I go away and I will come to you'
(Jn 14:18, 28); 'a little while, and you will see me no
more; again a little while, and you will see me' (Jn
16:16, 19).

It is by raising him up that God sends Christ into the
world; he destines him for us by raising him up. This
resurrection is wholly and entirely the salvation of men
and fullness for Christ, to such a point that it is impossible to distinguish in it the elements personal to Christ
from those which are salvific for mankind: 'Vindicated
in the Spirit' (1 Tim 3:16), 'made our righteousness' (1
Cor 1:30), 'raised for our justification' (Rom 4:25). The
resurrection is the universal coming of Christ for the
salvation of all, *it is the parousia* of which Jesus said, 'I
go away (by death), and I will come to you', a parousia
which one day will be realized in its fullness. Christ is
risen in himself and for this world: 'God having raised
up his servant, sent him to you . . ., to bless you' (Acts
3:26).[1]

The fourth gospel distinguishes in the unique reality
of the incarnation two aspects, sanctification in God and
mission to the world (Jn 10:36). In the glorifying death,
the incarnation reaches the fullness of its truth: sanctification is total, 'I consecrate myself' (17:19), and coming into the world is total, 'From now on I will come to

[1] For the identity of Christ's glorification and his parousia,
see F. X. Durrwell, *The Resurrection*, London and New York,
1960.

you' (cf 14:18). Glorifying death and parousia are two aspects of the incarnation in its fullness.

Man's salvation therefore is not played out in successive, separate acts, in which the redemption is first gained and then distributed. The salvation of all is achieved within the mystery of Christ, in the personal salvation that God realises in his Son. God does not distribute, nor does he repeat in each human being what he has accomplished in Christ: in effecting salvation in his Son, he extends it to men, effects it in men; in glorifying Christ, he sends him to them, brings them into union with him: 'Even when we were dead through our trespasses, he made us alive together with Christ . . ., and made us sit with him in the heavenly places in Christ Jesus' (Eph 2:5–6). According to Ephesians 1:19–22, the same action of God which exalts Christ to the pinnacle of all things constitutes him head of the church, creating the church in the glorification of Christ.

The church of the paschal Christ

The church is thus a part of the mystery of the paschal Christ: she is created in this mystery and remains enclosed in Christ and in the redemptive action. What Jesus asserts of himself, he says also of his church: she is sent like him and she is consecrated in his paschal consecration (Jn 17:18–19).

That coming of Christ into this world which is described in the words, 'I go away, and I will come to you', is realised through the intermediary of the church. It is in her that God raises up Christ in this world; she is the sacrament of the parousia of Christ in our world. Whatever is a means of salvation—the church herself, her apostles, her eucharists and all the other sacraments, as well as all apostolic activity—everything is at the service of the coming of Christ and depends on the action of God who, by glorifying Christ, sends him to men to subject them to his lordship of salvation. The apostolate is the mystery of Christ offered to men of this world so that they can take part in it.

It could not be otherwise. It is in Christ that God brings about men's salvation, it is in glorifying Christ that he concentrates all his saving power; from then onwards the apostolic action of the church can only be the manifestation of God's action in glorifying Christ himself. For men to be saved, it is Christ who must come, who must be preached, be revealed, be given to them.

The church is not only sent, she is consecrated: sent in so far as—immersed in Christ's redemptive consecration—she makes him present as the paschal Christ, the salvation of the world. For she is sent 'like' Christ (Jn 17:18), who is 'consecrated and sent'. The church is the saving presence of Christ for the world, because she lives in a union of salvation with Christ, sharing death and resurrection. She exercises her whole apostolate in this union, as St Paul did, regarding himself as delivered up to the death of Christ, 'so that the life of Jesus may be manifested in our mortal flesh and be at work in you' (2 Cor 4:11-12).

The church's apostolate therefore appears as inseparable from the church's holiness. It is for her what the work of the redemption was for Christ: a personal drama. Our Lord's redemptive task was not something added to his filial destiny, which consisted in going to the Father; the apostolate likewise cannot be dissociated from the church's vocation, called to unite herself to Christ in his pasch. From the time of the baptism of her faithful, in the labours of their faith, the demands of their charity, in their bounding hopes, and until death, the church takes part in the salvation of the world, wholly and entirely christian and apostolic, sanctifying herself and sanctifying men, by sharing in the death and resurrection of Christ.

4

AN APOSTOLIC CHURCH

In her profound, eschatological reality,[1] the church is one with the unity of God, with the unity of the Spirit of God and of the body of Christ (Eph 4:4-6); holy, with the holiness of the divine Spirit who is in Christ (Eph 5:25-27); catholic, according to the universality of salvation which is in Christ. These three *marks* characterize the church as an incarnate presence of God, as an extension of the presence of Christ into the world; they are the *marks* of the wonderful salvation already effected in the church and towards which she must tend.

In addition to these three there is another mark, at first sight a very human characteristic: twelve men have given her this name, the church is apostolic. Human as it may seem, this *mark* is one of profound richness; at one stroke, it brings us close to the heart of the mystery of the church. In order to be the presence in the world of Christ the *saviour*, it is not sufficient for her to be saved: in being saved, she must herself cause salvation.

The *mark* of apostolicity means that the church is linked with the first apostles by the unity of a history that has never been interrupted; it means that the

[1] Eschatology is not only a reality of the future, but the dimension of depth in christian existence: 'You have died, and your life is hid with Christ in God.' Eschatology is also a reality to come, because this dimension is still hidden from the christian until he shares fully in the reality: 'When Christ who is our life appears, then you also will appear with him in glory' (Col 3:3-4; cf. 1 Jn 3:2).

church is always this community built on the apostles, faithful to the essentials of her first structure, of her first teaching, of her first means of salvation. Apostolicity in the church is the mark of her fidelity to her origins. The word 'apostolic', however, has still another meaning which—in modern terminology—is the obvious one. Apostolicity means that the church is of her nature apostolic, wholly and entirely committed to the apostolate.[1] At the beginning, it was of apostles that she was made up and fidelity to her origins consists in continuing to be composed of apostles, of men who have the mission and the power to extend the salvation of Christ to the world.

I—A CHURCH COMPOSED OF APOSTLES

From the beginning of his preaching, Jesus had proclaimed the kingdom of heaven, described it in terms of a banquet prepared by the king for the marriage of his son. On the eve of his passion, he no longer proclaims it in words; he prepares the table and assembles the guests: 'As my Father appointed a kingdom for me, so do I appoint for you that you may eat and drink at my table in my kingdom' (Lk 22:29–30).

At the last supper the revelation of the kingdom reaches its peak of light and mystery: 'I have earnestly desired to eat this passover with you before I suffer; for I tell you I shall not eat it (this Jewish pasch) until it is fulfilled (that is to say, until I eat it in its reality) in the kingdom of God' (Lk 22:16). The kingdom of heaven

[1] 'The church has received from the apostles as a task to be discharged even to the ends of the earth this solemn mandate of Christ to proclaim the saving truth' (*The Church*, 17).

will bc a meal, but a paschal meal; not this Jewish pasch at which a lamb taken from the flock was eaten, but the pasch in all its truth: the mystery of the redemption celebrated by Christ with his disciples, of which the eucharistic meal is the sacramental realisation.

Fellow guests at this table are Christ and the apostles. It seems that there were no other guests at the supper. Luke relates on this occasion the saying: 'And you will sit on thrones judging the *twelve* tribes of Israel' (22:30). As defined by the eucharistic supper, the kingdom is composed of Christ and the apostles, gathered together at the celebration of the same redemptive pasch. Forever and in its totality the kingdom will be what it was defined at the last supper. The apostles therefore do not represent merely future bishops and future priests, but all the fellow guests of Christ's pasch, all the faithful of the kingdom:[1] does not this mean that the church always and in its totality will be composed of disciple-apostles?[2] Christ celebrates with his disciples forever the mystery of his pasch, that is to say, of the redemption: does this not mean that the church shares in the redemption of the world, that her activity lies there forever? The eucharist is the revelation of the mystery of the church, created in the fellowship of Christ, and of the apostolic character of this church.

When, after a night of prayer (Lk 6:12), Jesus took

[1] 'Jesus sees in the Twelve the representatives of the new people of God . . . They are the core of the new Messianic community'. J. Jeremias, *The Eucharistic Words of Jesus*, Oxford 1955, 139.

[2] It is true that the church, wholly and entirely apostolic, will be hierarchically organised in her apostolate. But the church is composed first and foremost of disciples who are apostles. She is church, apostolic church, prior to any differentiation in her apostolate.

the twelve aside, *it was not in order to separate them from the rest of the church*, but to place them at the head of the church—that is, at her source. For there was not yet a church from which they could have been set apart;[1] in them Christ was beginning to gather together his church: 'He called to him those whom he desired; and they came to him. And he appointed twelve, to be with him, and to be sent out to preach' (Mk 3:13–14). There had been twelve men at the origin of ancient Israel: these were 'the fathers' (cf Rom 9:5) and they became the people of the twelve tribes; like a seed, they grew and became one nation. The twelve companions of Jesus are at the origin of the new Israel;[2] the plant will grow, will become the church, the tree will remain faithful to its origins. The church of today is that of the twelve: not only because she was inaugurated by them, but because she is this plant now become a tree, the apostolic church.[3]

In the book of Revelation the church appears in the guise of a woman with a crown of twelve stars (ch.12), in the guise too of a city descending from heaven, provided with twelve gates, with ramparts measuring on every side twelve thousand stades and placed on twelve

[1] The kingdom was still a reality of the future (cf, among other texts, Lk 22:16) and therefore the church too, which on earth is the sacrament of the kingdom. By setting the twelve apart, Christ did not separate them from the other members of the church: in them he announced and prepared his church.

[2] 'The apostles were the first members of the New Israel' (*Missions*, 5).

[3] In addition to this fundamental symbolism of the number twelve, we should perhaps recall the fact that in antiquity twelve had always been a cosmic number (cf Rengstorff, *TDNT*, II, 325f.). This cosmic symbolism is emphasized in the image of the woman adorned with the sun, moon and twelve stars.

foundations, each of which bears the name of one of the twelve apostles of the Lamb and which are adorned with twelve precious stones (21:12–21). Until her final consummation, the number of the apostles remains the definition of the church.

It was in the perspective of the kingdom—which in the book of Revelation bears the name of 'City of the Lamb'—that Jesus placed the last supper which he celebrated with the disciples (cf Lk 22:14–20; Mk 14:25). Between the supper and this city the difference is that of a greater number of guests, the difference too which exists between a sacrament—an image which brings about of salvation—and salvation in its fullness. But the eucharist is at all times the image of the fullness of salvation: the kingdom is composed of Christ and his disciple-apostles who celebrate together the redemptive pasch.

II—A CHURCH POSSESSING AS A WHOLE A MISSION AND APOSTOLIC POWERS

To his disciple-apostles Christ entrusts a mission which is that of the whole church and confers on them powers which the whole church will exercise, since they were the representatives of the whole church in Christ's presence. It is true that Christ builds the church on the apostles alone and on Peter in particular; he charges them alone with the government of the messianic community: 'You will judge the twelve tribes of Israel' (Lk 22:30).[1] In all things the apostles are at the head and at the foundation.

Now this church on earth is always at her beginning

[1] 'Judge' must be understood here in the old semitic sense of 'rule' or 'govern' (cf Judg 2:16; Ruth 1:1; Amos 2:3; Wis 3:8).

and it is always 'on the foundation of the apostles' that God builds her. But, apart from this apostolic prerogative, there is certainly no word of Christ in scripture addressed to the apostles, no demand formulated in their regard, no power conferred, which is not the mission entrusted to the whole church, a charge on all the faithful, a power given to all. But this mission, these demands and these powers, concern the apostles and their successors the bishops in so far as they are at the foundation and at the head of the community.[1]

Involved in one and the same call

Jesus had grouped the twelve around him 'to be with him, and to be sent out to preach' (Mk 3:14). He gathered them together therefore to make them his disciples; St Matthew calls them *'the* twelve disciples' (10:1), or more simply *'the* disciples' (11:1; 14:19, 22; 15:32; 16:13), as if Christ did not include any others with them. But, according to Mark 8:34, he appeals to 'the multitude': 'If any man would come after me,' be my disciple. . . . The disciple follows Christ by sharing in his destiny. 'Follow me,' he says to Peter and he explains: 'You will stretch out your hand, and another will gird you and carry you where you do not wish to go' (to the torment of the cross) (Jn 21:18). Peter, who is at the head of the flock, is invited more pressingly than the others to imitate Christ. But every christian follows

[1] *Laity*, 2: 'The church carries on the apostolate in various ways through all her members . . . In the church, there is diversity of service but unity of purpose.' The apostolate is hierarchically organised, but not reserved to one group. Some are at the head of the community and therefore at the head of the apostolate; but they are not alone in the apostolate.

Christ by sharing his lot: 'Let him take up his cross and follow me' (Mk 8:34).[1]

The christian vocation and the apostolic vocation lead a man along one and the same path in following Christ, in sharing his redemptive destiny.

Sent on a mission

Jesus appoints the twelve 'to be sent out to preach'. After his resurrection, according to Acts 1:8, he sends them 'to the end of the earth'. From this moment onwards, the twelve are no longer alone in their preaching. Simultaneously with the extension of the community, the apostolic mission is widened. The first christians considered themselves apostles just because they were christians.[2] Persecution scatters them and with their dispersal the faith is propagated (Acts 11:19–21); warm-hearted women (Acts 16:14; Phil 4:2–3), christian families (Acts 18:26), lead their neighbours to Christ. At the end of the Epistle to the Romans there is a long list of christians devoted to the apostolate, all members of one and the same community: 'Prisca and Aquila, my fellow workers in Christ, . . . Andronicus and Junias, men of note among the apostles, . . . Mary who has worked hard among you, . . . Tryphaena and Tryphosa, workers in the Lord, . . . the beloved Persis, who has worked hard in the Lord' (16:1–16).

The apostles had been ordered to 'go into all the world' (Mk 16:15). A whole community—that of Antioch, for example—cannot set out for distant coun-

[1] 'To take up one's cross' means to follow Christ at the cost of one's life. 'Bearing the cross' had not yet become a metaphor for enduring life's trials. The early christians knew that faith in Christ could lead them to death.
[2] Cf The Church, 17; Laity, 2.

tries. The community at Antioch is nevertheless involved in the mission of Paul, Barnabas and Silas. These
apostles set out, '*commended by the brethren* to the grace of
the Lord' (Acts 15:40; cf. 13:1–3), and return to 'where
they had been commended to the grace of God for the
work which they had fulfilled' (Acts 14:26).

The christian preaches wherever he is, if he is a true
christian; and the fact of being a true christian is sufficient. 'You shall be my witnesses,' Christ had said to
the apostles (Acts 1:8), witnesses of his resurrection (1:
22). Every true christian is a witness, he makes 'the
glory of God' shine out, which is 'in the face of Christ'
(2 Cor 4:6), for 'we *all* reflect with, unveiled face (as in
a mirror), the glory of the Lord' (2 Cor 3:18). The light
which is in them is destined for the whole world: 'You
are the light of the world,' Jesus had said (Mt 5:14),
speaking to all his disciples.[1]

Ordered to celebrate the sacraments of salvation

The apostles' mission is to 'make disciples of all nations, baptising them' (Mt 28:19). But this baptism is
the work of the whole church, 'spouse of Christ, capable
of giving spiritual birth to children of God'.[2] Undoubtedly the decisive action and the invocation of God
on the neophyte were always reserved to the head of the
community,[3] but in the first age of christianity the
whole community was prepared 'by prayers and fasting'
for the celebration of the mystery[4] and took part in this:

[1] *The Church*, 33: 'Every layman, by virtue of the very gifts
bestowed upon him, is at the same time a witness and a
living instrument of the mission of the Church herself.'
[2] St Cyprian, *Ep.* 74, 6–7. *CSEL.*, 3, 2, 804.
[3] St Justin, *Apologies*, 1, 61. *PG* 6, col 420. Tertullian, *De
baptismo*, 17. *CCL* 1, 291.
[4] Apologies I, 61. *PG* 6, col 420.

'*We* however,' writes St Justin, 'after receiving the one who believes and who is united with us . . .'[1], for baptism 'is the work of the whole church, our mother, the assembly of the saints, since the whole church begets each and all of the baptized.'[2]

Christ orders the apostles: 'Do this in remembrance of me' (Lk 22:19). In the persons of the apostles all christians receive this mission and this power. In the eucharist, everyone, each in his own way, together with Christ, has to celebrate the mystery of the redemption.[3] Christ gives the 'disciples' (Mt 18:1; Jn 20:19) the power of binding and loosing, on earth and in heaven. He gives it first to Peter (Mt 16:19), on whom the community is founded, but the whole house only makes one with the foundation. The church as a whole shares in Peter's mission, since anyway she acquires solidity from the rock on which she is founded. The same saying is repeated later (Mt 18:18), but addressed to the 'disciples': 'Whatever you bind on earth shall be bound in heaven.' Here again the mission is entrusted to the apostles,[4] but in the context of a community ruling and to them as heads of a community of which they are themselves

[1] *op. cit.*, I, 65. *PG.* 6, col 428.
[2] St Augustine, *Ep.* 98, 5. *PL* 33, col 362: 'They are offered (for baptism), not so much by those who bear them in their hands (although in fact by them too if they are themselves good christians) as by the universal church.'
[3] *The Church*, 11: '(The faithful) both by the act of oblation and through holy communion, perform their proper act in this liturgical service . . . each in that way which is appropriate to himself.'
[4] It seems that this saying is addressed to the apostles, who are normally to be identified with the 'disciples' (Mt 18:1) in Matthew, at least from 10:1 onwards. It is to the leaders of the community that Christ recommends humility and solicitude for 'the little ones': this is evident from verses

members.[1] According to St John, the risen Christ shares his Spirit with the 'disciples', entrusting them *in this way* with his own mission of 'taking away the sin of the world': and we know that the whole church is entrusted with the gift of the Spirit who sanctifies the world.

Once introduced by the precursor as the one who would baptise the world in the Spirit, as the Lamb of God who would take away the sin of the world, Jesus became in very truth this lamb (Jn 19:36) when, in his immolation, he was consecrated in divine sanctity (Jn 17:19). Then there would spring from his side the fountains of the Spirit, announced on the Feast of Tabernacles (Jn 7:37–39) and in fact symbolized by the water which flowed from his wounded side. And wherever these waters spring up, sin is washed away, for the Spirit is divine holiness, remission of all sins.[2] It was then the evening of the Passover. St John, so attentive to the symbolism of numbers, who has inscribed the number seven on his whole gospel, observes that it was the first day of the week (20:19). It is the beginning of the septenary of the new creation, during which Christ acts as his Father had done and achieves a work greater than those he had effected on earth: the resurrection of the

12–14, of which verses 15–18 are the continuation. Cf Jeremias, *TDNT*, III, 751.

[1] This saying of Christ, related here in a collection of community rules, undoubtedly comes from another context. An exegete who has made a special study of Matthew 18 thinks that verse 18 is 'a promise and a mission given by the risen Christ to the apostles' (cf Jn 20:21–23). He adds 'and, by this very fact, given to all believers'. W. Pesch, *Matthäus der Seelsorger*, Stuttgart 1966, 37.

[2] 'The Spirit himself is the remission of all sins' (postcommunion of Tuesday of Pentecost).

dead. He had foretold it a long time before (5:20); but, before suffering, he announces that he will accomplish the greater works in his glory by means of the disciples (14:12). The breath of God which had once hovered above the waters of creation, the Spirit by whom all things are created, he imparts to his friends. He breathes on them and says to them: 'Receive the Holy Spirit.' Then he explains his intention: 'If you forgive the sins of any, they are forgiven' (20:22–23).

'The disciples' (20:19, 25), to whom the power of forgiving sins is given, are the same as the apostles (cf 20:24–25).[1] But there is nothing—particularly in the fourth gospel—to distinguish the apostles from the future disciples except that they constitute the beginning.[2] The gift of the Spirit, the power of holiness and remission of sins is not their exclusive privilege. Every believer, by the very fact of his faith, comes to draw on the Spirit at the fount of the Lord's heart (7:37–39); according to St Paul, the whole church in each of the faithful only makes one body with the Lord and shares with him the Spirit in whom he is glorified (1 Cor 6:17). Possessing the Spirit precisely as church and not only in some of her members, then as church and in all her faithful she has the mission and power to forgive sins: she is in her totality the sacrament of the remission of the sin of the world.

The church forgives sins in many ways: the word of Christ which she propagates and which is purifying (Jn 15:3), the sacraments she celebrates, her inter-

---

[1] From Chapter 13 onwards, Jesus' teaching mainly concerns the apostles.

[2] Augustine is right in saying that the words of John 20:22 are addressed to the whole church in the person of the apostles (*De baptismo* III, 18 n.23. *PL* 43, col 150).

cession, her own sanctification and her radiant charity, everything becomes for the others a source of the Holy Spirit, remission of sins in holiness.[1]

The church of the first centuries was aware of the role she had to play in all her faithful, including the sacramental reconciliation of sinners. It is true that the power of absolving was not exercised by all to the same extent, for the community was hierarchically organised;[2] nevertheless, in sacramental penance, it was in fact exercised by all. By its fervour of prayer and fasting, the whole community prepared the penitents for conversion and, in its charity, received those who wanted to take their place again in its midst. The church as a whole is the place of the Spirit and of forgiveness of sins and as a whole she receives men in grace; that is why St Augus-

[1] *The Church*, 11: The whole church, 'by charity, example and prayer, seeks their (sinners') conversion.' According to St Augustine (*Tract. in Ep. Joh.* x, 10, *PL* 35, col 2062), 'Where sin is forgiven, there is the church'. It could likewise be said: where the church in her authenticity is present, there is forgiveness of sins. It is true too up to a point that the christian's sin wrongs everyone: 'A single sinner tarnishes the people . . . One who committs fornication or another crime casts a stain on the whole people' (Origen, *Homily* vii, 6, *on Joshua. PG* 12, col 861).

[2] With reference to the penitential practice of the first centuries, K. Delahaye writes: 'As far as it is a form used by the church for mediating salvation, penance is also in principle the affair of all believers, even though the way in which the people act is different from that of the bishop . . . The nature of the cooperation (of the faithful) in carrying out penance is essentially personal. It has no sort of institutional character . . . This mediatory function of salvation belonging to the people as a whole is never regarded as autonomous and independent of the bishop, but to be exercised exclusively in association with him . . . Admission of penitents is the concern of the bishop or—at his order—of the priest' (*Ecclesia Mater*, Paris 1964, 239–241).

tine could say: 'It is not he alone (Peter), but the whole church that binds and looses sins.'[1]

This reception, in which formerly the co-operation of all in the forgiveness of sins was visibly expressed, ought unceasingly to be that of the christian in forgiving offences, in the friendship offered to all the people he meets. In this charity the church is already open to men, the love of Christ which is in the church already fills them, destines them and will lead them to an absolute charity which is forgiveness of sins. Jesus forgave, Stephen forgave, and they offered their persecutors the grace of reconciliation in the Holy Spirit. From the moment it is accepted, the christian's friendship is for the other person forgiveness of sins or at least a beginning of this forgiveness.

The spiritual care of the sick is something for which

[1] *In Johannem, tract.* 124, 7. *CCL* 36, p. 687. In several other texts also, St Augustine asserts that the whole church shares in the forgiveness of sins: 'Who binds then? Who binds then? I venture to say: we have these keys, we also (we the bishops). And what am I saying? That we bind? That we loose? You too bind (you, the laypeople), you too loose. In fact, he who is bound is separated from your community; he is bound by you. And when he is reconciled, he is loosed by you, because God receives your prayers also for him.' *Sermo Guelferb.* 16, 2. ed. G. Morin, I, 493. Cf *In Johannem tract.* 124, 5, *CCL* 36, 684.

In a study of J. A. Möhler, a theologian writes: 'Forgiveness of sins is the work of the community of the faithful . . . Every true christian has a power of forgiving sins' (J. R. Geiselmann, *Die theologische Anthropologie Johann Adam Moehlers*, Freiburg 1955, 48–49). The naive, but expressive words of St Teresa of Lisieux might be quoted here: 'How proud I was when it was my turn to lead the office for a week and to say aloud the prayers in the centre of the choir! I thought of the fact that the priest said the same prayers at Mass and that I had—like him—the right to speak in the presence of the Blessed Sacrament, to give blessings and absolutions' (*Novissima Verba*, Lisieux 1926, 123).

Saint James demands the interest of the whole community, while reserving a primary role for the presbyters (5:14–16). Vatican II gives a faithful interpretation of this text: 'By the sacred anointing of the sick and the prayer of her priests, the whole Church commends those who are ill to the suffering and glorified Lord, asking that he may lighten their suffering and save them.'[1]

To sum up: all the sacraments are sacraments of the whole church, rooted in the church as primordial sacrament, celebrated in her and by her. 'Where am I to eat the passover with my disciples?' (Mk 14:14), Jesus had asked. The passover which is redemption he celebrates with his disciples for ever. The eucharist, theological image of the church, is a communion with Christ in the work of the redemption. The church is composed of those who share with Christ in his death and his resurrection: it belongs to her very nature to co-operate in the salvation of the world.

III—A MOTHER CHURCH[2]

The christian community from the very beginning had been aware of the fruitfulness in eternal life with which God had endowed it. The apostle testifies to this at a very early date when he speaks of 'the Jerusalem above, our mother' (Gal 4:26); the johannine writings have exploited this image of the church's motherhood in a variety of ways.

It was once thought possible to discern an opposition between the johannine theology of salvation on the one hand and the synoptic thought on the kingdom with the

[1] *The Church*, 11.
[2] Cf *The Church*, 64; *Priests*, 6.

pauline doctrine of the church on the other; 'the individualism of the johannine theology of salvation' was heavily underlined. It is true that the author of the fourth gospel insists more than others on the personal character of salvation, but nevertheless John is a great theologian of the ecclesial community: he shows 'a lively and burning interest'[1] in its missionary activity and even offers us, from chapter 12 onwards, a very coherent charter of the apostolate.

The high priest reaches his decision on the death of Jesus, 'not for the nation only, but to gather into one the children of God who are scattered abroad' (11:52). The time of signs has passed: the hour of 'greater things' has arrived, the hour which is that of Christ (5:20f.) and with which the disciples will be associated (14:12). Jesus enters Jerusalem, anticipating in sign—by a week, to be exact—the inauguration of his reign. The Jewish crowds come out to meet him and the Greeks too are now trying to approach him: Jews and pagans thus bring Caiaphas' prophecy to the beginning of its fulfilment. When Jesus learns of the step taken by the pagans, a feeling of joy comes over him: 'The hour has come,' he says, 'for the Son of man to be glorified' (Jn 12:23). Now the time is near when the servant 'shall be exalted and lifted up, and shall be very high' (Is 52:13) and will be glorified in 'the many' whom God will assign to him (Is 53:11–12), glorified by a proliferation of life like that of the grain of wheat. This glory, already coming upon Jesus, tells him at the same time of the closeness of death: an exorbitant exaltation, an exaltation above the earth, on the cross. 'When I am lifted up from the earth, I will draw all men

[1] R. Schnackenburg, *New Testament Theology Today*, London 1963, 100.

to me' (Jn 12:32). The community of salvation will be established in the immolated Christ: the heavy ear of wheat which is born from the sacrificed grain is Christ himself transformed by death.

Jesus had not yet however reached the full truth of his existence, was not yet glorified. The redemptive mission, the gathering together in him of the children of God, is demanded by his filial nature. He is 'the word' addressed to men for their salvation,[1] God's saving plan being put into effect in the world; he is the beloved Son in as much as he is delivered up for salvation (Jn 10:17); he is the Lamb of God consecrated to God by death and given in a communion of life. He had not yet reached his hour, not yet come to himself.

Jesus attributes to himself the name that God had once given himself: 'I am' (Ex 3:14). He says: 'Before Abraham was, I am' (8:58). But most often he makes this transcendence functional, states that his greatness is asserted in the salvation of the world: 'I am the bread of life' (6:35), 'I am the good shepherd' who 'lays down his life . . . that they may have life' (10:10–11), 'I am the true vine' (15:1). Christ is of himself the salvation of the world—'I am the resurrection' (11:25)—so much so that his mystery is realised and revealed only in the work of salvation: 'When you have lifted up the Son of man, you will know that I am he' (8:28).

Jesus will be glorified in a community of salvation gathered together in him. The glory of the grain is the ear into which it is transformed: 'The hour has come for the Son of man to be glorified. Truly, if a grain of wheat

[1] In St John the Word is not only the word that God speaks to himself, but perhaps mainly the word—immanent, it is true (1:1)—that God pronounces for creation and salvation.

dies it bears much fruit'. Jesus will rise as a temple in which the new people is assembled (2:19–21); he will be the true vine whose branches bear much fruit. On the eve of the passion, he prays: 'Father, glorify thy Son, since thou hast given him power over all flesh, to give eternal life to all' (17:1–2). Christ will be glorified when, in himself, he gives life. This paradoxical johannine doctrine of a Christ of glory, a being who is unique and communal, is the faithful development of the concise synoptic doctrine of the kingdom which 'comes' in the glorification of the Son of man. Jesus becomes wholly and entirely the kingdom, as an early writer puts it.[1]

The church, a vine

Jesus initiated his disciples into the mystery of his redemptive existence. In the discourses at the last supper he speaks to 'his own' (13:1), to those whom 'he loved to the end', the apostles.[2] But in Christ's view the apostles are not distinguished from the church as a whole. To these twelve, who represent the whole church, Jesus declares: 'You did not choose me, but I chose you and appointed you that you should go and bear fruit and that your fruit should abide' (15:16). Christ's choice destines these men to be apostles;[3] he has 'appointed' them, in-

[1] Origen, *In Matth.*, 14, 7.
[2] According to the synoptic tradition, the only guests at the supper were the twelve. Moreover, it certainly seems that in John 13:1–11 we are meeting again the same persons as in John 6:67–71 (with a special mention of Peter and Judas), in a similar situation (loyalty to Christ or betrayal), in a similar framework (eucharistic discourse, last supper). And in John 6:67–71 it is a question of the twelve.
[3] The verb 'to choose' always has this meaning in St John (cf 6:70; 13:18; 15:16, 19). See Schrenk, *TDNT*, IV 178.

vesting them with a mission,[1] the object of which is to 'go', bearing the message[2] and yielding fruit, the fruit of the apostolate.

Christ had just said: 'I am the true vine, . . . you are the branches. He who abides in me, and I in him, he it is that bears much fruit' (15:1, 5). Scripture had once given Israel the name of God's vine, a vine that sometimes produced good fruit for its Master, but most often did not. In these texts there is no point in asking about the precise meaning of these fruits; the vine is true or false to the extent of their abundance or shortage: the true vine of God is the vine that bears fruit. In the allegory of John 15:1–10, if the whole context were not apostolic, it might be thought that the fruits had no precise meaning: they would simply prove the fidelity of the branches. Many authors think that the fruits are a symbol of the good works of the believer, an expression of fidelity to the commandments. The context, it seems, compels us to give a more precise meaning to the fruits. While having a universal import, the discourse is addressed to the apostles. Moreover, the expression 'bear much fruit' (15:5, 8) is found elsewhere with the meaning of fruits of redemption (12:24). The fruits borne by the branches are for the glory of God (15:8), just as Christ himself is glorified in the fruits of redemption (12:23–24). In 14:12 it is a question of greater works that the apostles will achieve in the glorified Christ, recalling those greater works to which—according to 5:20f. —Christ knew he was destined and which consist in raising men for eternal life: might not 'the fruit that

[1] The verb 'to appoint' normally suggests a function. Cf Acts 20:28; 1 Cor 12:18.
[2] In the verb 'to go' there is an allusion to sending (Jn 17:18; 20:21).

abides', produced by the vine through its branches, be understood precisely of this same work of eternal life? In any case, if there is any ambiguity, it is removed by verse 16. Père Lagrange was right to see there 'the key to this whole discourse' and in this discourse 'a programme of the apostolate'.[1]

The image of the vine contains a profound theology of the apostolate. Christ is both the vine stock and the whole vine: the existence of 'his own' is immanent to himself (15:5) and the fruits produced by his own are also immanent. Elsewhere Jesus calls himself the resurrection of men (11:25), the bread of their eternal life, the one who gives life to all flesh (17:2); the task which he pursues through his disciples, that which is proper to him, is not only the observance of the commandments, but a fructification of eternal life. 'The church bears much fruit, namely, those who are saved.'[2] Christ takes her into his own salvific existence and constitutes with her one single principle generative of eternal life.

When we bring together the images of the grain of wheat and the vine, the church's apostolate is seen in an incomparable light. It is in the church that the filial glory of Christ is displayed, expressed in fruits of salvation; God glorifies Christ in the church; Christ bears fruit in the church; belonging to Christ means bearing abundant fruit in souls: 'By this my Father is glorified, that you bear much fruit, and so prove to be my disciples' (15:8). The disciple bears fruit in virtue of the demands of his very existence as disciple; any sterile branch is cut off—'any branch that bears no fruit, (God) takes away'—for it does not remain in him who—by his

[1] *Evangile selon saint Jean*, Paris 1927, 408.
[2] Irenaeus, *Proof of the Apostolic Preaching*, 94.

nature—is source and apportionment of eternal life. 'Woe to me if I do not preach the gospel' is a threat that hangs over every christian. Does this mean for a christian that the criterion of the authenticity of his life lies in the *visible* success of the apostolate? It is in his death, beyond his earthly life, that Christ sees the fruits of his redemption: the fruits which abide are eternal realities and they elude the criteria of this world.

A city

In addition to that of the vine loaded with grapes, scripture has other images, also maternal in character. One such is the image of the city fruitful in numerous children. In biblical thought, a city is the mother of its inhabitants: they are born in it, it bears them in its womb. Sion, the messianic city, more than any other, is maternal, a metropolis of the nations. One day, when compiling the register of peoples, God will enter against each nation the note: 'This one was born there; that one was born there.' And each of the peoples will say to her, 'Mother', for in her each one is born (Ps 87; cf. Is 54:1–7; 66:7–13). But 'our mother, the Jerusalem above,' is the church (Gal 4:26). The book of Revelation underlines the maternal significance in which the image itself is already rich and shows 'the river of life' spurting forth in the midst of the 'holy city' (22:1), with the tree of life on either side, 'yielding its fruit each month' and whose leaves are 'for the healing of the nations' (22:2).

A christian woman, representative of the whole church

John's gospel gives a final, definitive image of the maternal church, one that will never be eclipsed. His theology is made up of intuitions and—in order to preserve the inner splendour of the mystery—is expressed more frequently in significant images than in abstract concepts. The gospel speaks on two occasions of 'the mother of Jesus' (2:1; 19:25); this maternal title alone is used, while the synoptics refer to her by her name of Mary. Contrary to what one would expect of a son, Jesus calls her by a theological name, the name of her function. Twice he calls her 'Woman' (2:4; 19:26), recalling the one who was given at the beginning of things the name of woman, 'the mother of all living'.[1]

This woman is Mary, mother of Jesus; but she is the holy image of the church, the church in her pure truth.[2] In Revelation (c.12) the text on the Woman, the mother of Jesus, is to be understood primarily in its ecclesial sense. The image of the woman who gives life to children, nurtures and educates them, expresses with so much truth the mission of the christian community that it was impressed on the mind of everyone who spoke about the church during the first centuries. Inspired by the pauline and johannine theologies, the Fathers saw the church as a bride, united to Christ in one single body and through him fruitful in eternal life for all.

The ancient authors see a grandiose role for the church. As in the book of Revelation, they see her adorned with all the stars, crying in labour, bringing all Christ's brethren into the world. She is not merely the handmaid of her Lord, charged with children to rear. Undoubtedly, she 'nurses and takes care' of them (cf

---

[1] The book of Revelation recalls still more clearly the memory of Eve, since, opposite the woman who is mother of Christ, there stands the dragon, 'the ancient serpent' (12:9).
[2] *The Church*, 63–65.

1 Thess 2:7), but she is more than nurse: she is first and foremost *genetrix*, 'she who is perpetually in labour'.[1]

Each local church and each believer in particular may assume completely this maternal mission undertaken by the universal church. For the church's mission is undivided and cannot be distributed in separate parts to smaller communities and to each of the faithful. The law of communion which governs the christian reality means that Christ does not divide his work of salvation into parts, but entrusts it entirely to his church; it means that the church is not split up into the multitude of her particular communities and of her faithful, but is wholly and entirely in each one of them. Beginning from Christ, its centre, the mystery of salvation extends in ever widening circles: 'The church is whole and entire in each.'[2]

It is in this way that the local church to which John's second epistle is addressed is the chosen of God and the mother of the faithful within her (vv.1, 4, 13). Such is the privilege of every christian community, as far as it is authentic, the privilege of the 'domestic church' which each christian family constitutes[3] and of every christian

[1] K. Delahaye, *op. cit.*, p. 175. This is how St Hippolytus comments on Revelation 12:2: 'She cries in the pangs of childbirth, for the church never ceases to bear children' (*De Antichristo*, 61).

[2] *Ecclesia . . . in singulis tota, in suis partibus tota* (St Peter Damian, *Opusc. XI. Dominus vobiscum*, 5 and 6, *PL* 145, col 235). St Paul seems to make a distinction by dividing up the activities of the church in terms of the different roles played by the members of the body (1 Cor 12). But at the same time he insists on the participation of all in the same work. In 1 Corinthians 6:16f., he recognises in the individual believer the privilege of the whole church of being the body of Christ.

[3] *The Church*, 11.

grouping or 'movement': according to the intensity of its faith and of its communal charity, each community contributes to bringing its members to birth in the life of Christ.

Such, finally, is the privilege of each believer. It was in this way that the apostle Paul, himself born of the church and reared by her, became—as Methodius of Olympus puts it—church in his turn and knew the 'labours of childbirth for those who came to believe in the Lord through him, until Christ was formed and born. Doesn't he say: "My little children, with whom I am again in travail until Christ be formed in you" (Gal 4:19), and "I begot you in Christ Jesus through the gospel" (1 Cor 4:15).'[1]

This faith in the maternal mission of each believer had a considerable repercussion in the churches of the martyrs. The letter of the christians of Lyons, at the end of the second century, speaks of believers who by their faith and their goodness gave life as a mother does to their brethren who at first had lapsed in face of persecution; it tells of a christian doctor, concerned with the fidelity of his brethren, so that 'he seemed to those present to be suffering the pains of childbirth for them'; of Blandina who 'roused the zeal of her brethren, although she was small, weak and despised, for she had been clothed with Christ, the mighty and invincible athlete,' and, after all the others, 'as a noble mother, having encouraged her children and sent them before

---

[1] *The Banquet* III, 9, *PG* 18, col 76. According to Methodius, this spiritual maternity is proper to every christian whose faith is mature: 'The best, those who have already better assimilated the lights of truth, . . . become the church and Christ's aid, . . . his spouses, . . . in order to co-operate in the salvation of others' (*op. cit.*, III, 8. *PG* 18, col 73).

her victorious to the king, herself endured all their conflicts.'[1]

This faith in the spiritual maternity of believers has been handed down through the centuries of christian sanctity and, ever and again, by the grace of the Spirit, which is the fruitfulness of God, it is born in the heart of many of the faithful and becomes the daily stimulant of their generosity. The role played by this faith in life of Teresa of Lisieux from her adolescence onwards is well known. Teresa did not want to be simply a mother of souls, but '*the* mother of souls'. Across the centuries, she rediscovered the bold language of the first ages of christianity and the desire to live the vocation of the whole church, to be in this way the heart of the church, the church of all time and of the whole world concentrated in her heart: 'To be your bride, O Jesus . . . to be through my union with you *the* mother of souls!'[2] The heart of great christians has always been a very great city, a metropolis of souls.

IV—CHRISTIANS AND APOSTLES

No one then is ever a christian for himself alone. The title of 'disciples' in the gospel often simply means the apostles and nothing else: those who are '*the* disciples'. It seems in fact that Jesus, after the first stages of his preaching, reduced the circle of the disciples, at first larger and more fluctuating, to the definitive group of the twelve.[3] This is evident from a number of scriptural

[1] Eusebius, *Ecclesiastical History* v, 1, 41–55. *PG* 20, coll 425–432.
[2] 'Manuscrits autobiographiques', ed. *Livre de vie*, Lisieux 1957, 223.
[3] 'At the beginning, "disciples" was the name given to all those who heard the word of Jesus . . . and who, by their

indications, which lead to the conclusion that there are no disciples other than apostles associated with Christ in his messianic work. Jesus will go as far as to say that his sacrifice is intended to create apostles: 'As thou didst send me into the world, so I have sent them (I send them) into the world. And for their sake I consecrate myself (in the redemptive death), that they also may be consecrated' (Jn 17:18–19). Every christian is baptised in this consecration, that which creates apostles.

We see Christ then giving to his own a name, not of disciples who hear and believe, but of a function, of co-operation: 'If anyone *serves* me, he must follow me; and where I am, there shall my *servant* be also; if anyone serves me, the Father will honour him' (Jn 12:26). Jesus had just invited his own to 'lose their life' and, like himself, to die as the grain of wheat dies (vv.24–26). According to the synoptics, this invitation is addressed to every disciple (cf Mk 8:34–37); the impersonal expression 'if anyone' has a very general bearing, as in the synoptics. All believers therefore are invited to this 'service'. But it is not a question of a service to be rendered to the person of Christ, who 'came not to be served' (Mt 20:28; Lk 22:26–27; Jn 13:12–15): in this context of the Hour and of the fruitfulness of Jesus' death, there can be a question only of a ministry in the service of Christ in his redemptive function. To be a disciple, therefore, is to be in the service of the redeeming Christ.

---

faith, declared themselves for him as being the Messiah . . . This originally wider and still fluctuating group of disciples Jesus in all probability reduced definitively to the symbolic number of twelve' (H. Schümrann, 'Le groupe des disciples de Jesus, signe pour Israel et prototype de la vie selon les conseils' in *Christus* 13 (1966), p. 184.

God does not grant all men during their life on earth the privilege of faith in Christ, nor that of baptism and the eucharist, the privilege of an anticipated membership of the eschatological kingdom. And yet he is the God who 'shows no partiality' (Rom 2:11; Eph 6:9), Father of every man for eternal life, creator for salvation. The filial grace already given on earth, christian grace, is intended for the salvation of the world. Jesus is both Son of God and saviour, all his filial grace is expressed in the gift of himself for the life of men; he is the beloved Son of God in so far as he is saviour: 'For this reason the Father loves me, because I lay down my life, that I may take it again' (Jn 10:17). Salvation then is not a grace to be enjoyed in solitude: it consists in fellowship with Christ, Son of God, saviour of the world. The christian privilege is not a monopoly from which other men are excluded, a principle which would divide humanity: this grace is given to some in order to gather together all men in the same grace.

5

HOLY AND APOSTOLIC

The apostolic mission was not entrusted to the church in the form of a simple precept. The christian is no longer subject to a rule imposed by a set of commandments: 'Now we are discharged from the law'(Rom 7:6). It is true that some precepts remain and are indeed enjoined on us by scripture: 'This is my commandment, that you love one another', 'they ought always to pray and not lose heart' (Lk 18:1), among other precepts. But it is a question of formulating requirements imposed by the very nature of the christian life, of a necessary reminder to us who are sinners, not sufficiently sensitive to our interior 'anointing' (1 Jn 2:20) or to the utterly pure voice of grace. The law is also brought home to us from outside, in as much as we are still sinners (1 Tim 1:9). Apostolic activity is immanent to grace, it is the dynamism of sanctity, the incoercible and often mysterious radiation of the christian reality. The christian soul lives and breathes by its apostolic desire and charity.[1]

Holy by sharing in the redemption

The apostolate cannot be dissociated from the mystery of Christ in which we share for our sanctification and which is the mystery of the world's redemption. In a juridical theology of redemption, the salvation of a man

[1] Vatican II, *Missions*, 2: 'The church is missionary by her very nature.' *Laity*, 2: 'By its very nature the christian vocation is also a vocation to the apostolate.'

concerns that man alone. By his death, Christ has paid the price of sin and obtained grace. Henceforward, God 'applies' forgiveness and grace to those who believe in him and in his redeeming death; man benefits from the gift that God grants, but he has no part in the work of salvation itself in Jesus Christ: he receives, he is passive, the salvation received is for him alone.

How much more expressive of the complexity of the mystery is the thought of the first theologians of the redemption, of St Paul and St John, for whom Christ opened up the way when he instituted the eucharist: sacrament, not of application of merits, but of fellowship with Christ in his merit. They say that men's salvation is completely achieved in Christ and in him alone, in his death, in which he is glorified; that men are saved when they share with him in this personal salvation, uniting themselves to him in his glorifying death. The merit of Christ is not 'applied' or 'distributed' to them. It cannot be, since it is personal to Christ, since it is Christ himself in his death by which he receives the saving glory of the Father. But, by the grace of God, man can share in this merit by uniting himself to Christ in his glorifying death. He cannot share in it in a passive receptivity, for this merit is an action of sovereign freedom, the total welcome given to the Father by Christ for the salvation of the world. Man enters into it by participation: he is saved when he takes part in the mystery of the world's redemption.

Christian existence lies at the heart of the mystery of the redemption. In order to become a son of God, man unites himself to Christ when the latter enters into his filial plenitude, when he becomes the perfect image of the Father, when Christ dies for the life of the world. It is there that Christ is head of the church, his body, and it is there that man becomes christian: in redemptive self-sacrifice. There is no encounter with salvation except in Christ and in his Hour. St Paul uses two formulas to define christian existence: 'in Christ' and 'with Christ'. The first means that christian existence is fellowship with Christ, the second that it is participation in the death and resurrection. These two requirements of christian existence go together: 'You have come to fullness of life in him, . . . you were buried with him in baptism, in which you were also raised with him' (Col 2:10–12). The church is holy and therefore saved to the extent that she participates in the salvation of the world.

On the eve of his passion, Jesus had gathered together his own at the paschal meal, had associated them with himself in his body that was given and in his blood that was shed. Henceforward, they are really 'his own', by sharing in the body and blood (cf 1 Cor 10:16). But this body is given and the blood is shed 'for many'. They are taken up into the redemptive existence of Christ, and it is in this way that they are christians. It has often been repeated that the christian has no right to be saved alone. In fact, he cannot be. He is saved in a community of salvation with Christ, in Christ's death which is salvific for all. An isolated christian, closed up against the salvation of others, would himself be excluded from salvation.

We must then get away from a theology which presents Christ as distributing through the church the graces acquired once and for all. The church is not a means of distribution, she is not even a handmaid: the church is the bride, united to Christ and associated in the work of salvation which is inseparable from the person of

Christ; her role is that of Christ.[1] Like Christ, but in complete subordination to him, so too the church can be said to be the cause of salvation. Christ does not associate his own with his work in order to complete it: the church is not added to Christ, she is identified with him, she is his body. She adds nothing to the merit of Christ's death and nothing to the power of his resurrection: she receives all this, she is the receptive 'fullness' of Christ (Eph 1:23; Col 2:9), filled with the presence of Christ and of his redemptive action. His merit is not parallel to that of the church, the paschal mystery is the same in Christ and in the church.

If the church's action were merely complementary, it would prove that Christ's action is defective, in need of completion;[2] the church's action is total, at its own level. The unique paschal mystery in its entirety is lived both by Christ and by his bride, the church: the church which is Christ's own body in one and the same death and resurrection. And this unique mystery may be described as redemption or apostolate, as it is seen in the person of Christ or in the church. But it is also possible to speak of the apostolate of Christ (Heb 3:1; cf Jn 10:36) and the redemption accomplished by the church in her apostolate.

[1] Patristic theology was fond of calling her 'the companion' of Christ, his 'helper', alluding to her who was created to be the helper of the first man (Gen 2:18). Cf, for example, Clement of Alexandria, *The Pedagogue*, 1, *PG* 8, col. 277.

[2] To say that the church complements the work of Christ would contradict the whole of pauline thought. However Colossians 1:24 is to be translated, exegetes are unanimous in interpreting the text in a way that does not contradict this principle. The usual translation is: 'In my flesh I complete what is lacking *in* Christ's afflictions.' But it could and undoubtedly should be translated: 'I complete what is lacking in my flesh *of* Christ's afflictions.'

Apostolic through her holiness

For the church, the apostolate will always consist in being herself faithful, in being the bride united to her Lord, making one body with him in his glorifying death. It is in this way that the fruits of salvation which God produces in Christ are produced in her.[1]

Undoubtedly, Christ and the salvation that is in him must be proclaimed in a variety of ways. But this proclamation will never be anything but the celebration of the paschal mystery among men, so that they can take part in it. The eucharistic meal is the eternal image of the church and also of her activity, which will always consist in living in communion with Christ in his mystery of salvation and in expressing this communion by living it.[2] The whole christian life is therefore apostolic,[3] for the whole christian life in its authenticity is communion with Christ.

Already in believing, already in submitting to baptism, man is consecrated in the redemptive pasch which, according to John 17:18–19, creates apostles. He abandons himself and abandons everything for Christ's sake, in principle and already in fact, for faith enrols man in the following of Christ on the way of his cross, that is, of his death: baptism is a sharing in Christ's death (Rom

[1] According to patristic thought, the church need only be herself in order to be fruitful. 'For Origen as for Hippolytus' —other writers of the first centuries might also be quoted— 'the church is a mother who bears children, because Christ never ceases to unite himself to her in an act of conjugal union, so that, thanks to this union, sons and daughters will be given to God from him and by her' (K. Delahaye, *Ecclesia Mater*, Paris 1964, 175–176).

[2] Preaching itself is nothing but this communion in faith and its expression.

[3] Cf *The Church*, 34.

6:3). Thus the saying that holds for the apostles holds too for every disciple: he who has left everything 'for my sake and for the gospel' (Mk 10:29).[1] It always is in the service of the gospel that the disciple follows Christ, faith is itself an apostolate.[2] When the christian sinner immerses himself again in the redemptive mystery by submitting to the 'baptism of pain', to penance, his conversion no less than his sin is never without repercussions in the world. He rises and goes to his Father (Lk 15:18), with Christ who rose in his pasch (Jn 14:31) and went 'out of this world to the Father' (Jn 13:1). And any participation in Christ's pasch rebounds on others in effects of salvation.

It has been said of the eucharistic celebration that it is 'the apex of the whole work of preaching the gospel'.[3] This it is, not because of its value as preaching—'you proclaim the Lord's death until he comes' (1 Cor 11:26) —but much more because christians are there created apostles, as at the last supper, and because the church there becomes even more of a community of redemption in her Lord.[4] Celebrated in truth, the eucharist brings

[1] 'For the sake of the gospel' is an addition proper to St Mark. But the perspective is likewise apostolic in the parallel texts of Matthew and Luke ('for my name's sake', 'for the sake of the kingdom'). The disciple follows Christ in his person and for his sake.
[2] St Paul speaks of 'being baptized on behalf of the dead' (1 Cor 15:29). The nature of this practice remains obscure. Some thought that it was a baptism received in the hope of benefiting relations who had died as pagans. Probably it is a question of a baptism received by pagans wanting to rejoin one day christian friends or relatives who had died. Cf J. Jeremias, *Infant Baptism in the First Four Centuries*.
[3] *Priests*, 5.
[4] Methodius of Olympus thinks that God's order to increase and multiply is carried out especially when the church is

christians together where Christ is, at the heart of the world, in his death for the world.[1]

When the faithful celebrate the sacrament of their marriage together in their conjugal life—for the whole of a conjugal life lived in faith is a sacramental celebration, sign and realisation of the love of Christ and the church—it is the mystery of salvation they are celebrating.[2] Their home becomes the church of Christ in the mystery of salvation, the small but real 'domestic church',[3] capable of putting into effect—often in an astonishing fruitfulness of grace—the ecclesial mission of giving eternal life. Here, each one is an apostle,[4] not

---

united to her Lord in the eucharist (*The Banquet* III, 8, *PG* 18, col. 73).

[1] In the past, devout people sometimes spoke of receiving communion for someone. This was not entirely an empty formula, although it could not mean the same as saying mass for someone. However inappropriate, the language of real devotion—that is, of faith and charity—is always meaningful. The christian never takes part alone in the mystery of salvation and he 'communicates' all the more for others in so far as his fraternal charity seeks to grow greater.

[2] There are seven sacraments by which God creates the church; but, at a deeper level, the church herself is the sacrament of salvation, sign and cause of salvation. Every more limited church, such as the christian family which is the domestic church, shares in this sacramentality.

The sacraments are at the service of this sacramentality of the church; once received, they continue to be celebrated in some way in the permanent sacrament, the church. Tertullian says that we are reborn in the water of baptism, but we are saved only by remaining in it (*De baptismo* I, 3. *CCL* I, 277). The sacrament of marriage likewise, in which the domestic church is created, continues to be celebrated.

[3] *The Church*, 11.

[4] According to St Augustine (*In Joh. tract.* 51, 13. *CCL* 36, 445), the father of the family exercises 'so to speak, an episcopal function': 'Therefore, brethren, when you hear the

only by force of example, but because the family never ceases to be gathered together in the mystery of the redemption.

The sacraments—especially the eucharist—have as their object to make the whole life of the church a celebration of the redemptive sacrifice. Throughout his life as an apostle, St Paul was aware of being crucified with Christ and living by his new life (Gal 2:20). The faithful believe and pray, are poor in spirit and rise to pure charity in Christ as he goes to his Father: with Christ, they accept inevitable suffering (Rom 8:17) until the day of their death when they enter with Christ into total communion of redemptive death and glory (2 Tim 2:11). The mystery of the redemption is always celebrated in the church. The christian's labours may well remain hidden, but the energy of grace is always generating life: in every work of salvation, the church becomes a mother of men.

It is of course by the visible testimony of faith, by the visible radiance of charity, that the church as visible sacrament of salvation is propagated. Since she belongs to a world of sensible things, the church is true, faithful to the love of all men, only by living and proclaiming her faith and love in face of the world and in striving to

---

Lord saying, "Where I am, there too my servant will be," don't think only of good bishops and clerics. You too in your own way minister to Christ, proclaiming his name and doctrine to whom you can, so that any father also may admonish, teach, exhort, correct his family, lavish good will and impose discipline on them. Thus in his home he will exercise an ecclesial and in a way an episcopal function, ministering to Christ in order to be eternally with him.' These last words mean that we are with Christ through the ministry we exercise, that grace and apostolate are inseparable.

spread 'to the end of the earth'. Nevertheless, she has never yet reached this limit and undoubtedly never will. The apostolate is bound to be marked with the sign of the cross, since it is exercised in communion with Christ in his death, a death that could not be counted as success. In the universal triumph of her apostolate, does the church share in Christ's defeat? The church is created, not for defeat, but for the salvation of all men: as with Christ himself, defeat is also resurrection. The apostolate possesses a dimension of depth through which the church can reach the hearts of all men and prepare them for the kingdom: she is for all men the sacrament of the kingdom, the kingdom of eternity which, beyond the vicissitudes of her earthly history, is the church's one solid hope. The leaven in the world is invisible, the church for the most part is invisible and totally invisible in her deeper workings. But, through her presence in the world, through her fidelity, the weight of the redeeming Christ presses on the deep centre of humanity, turning it towards himself: 'I will draw all men to myself.' When and by what ways will those so drawn come to him? God has not revealed this. But it is certain that, having become one being with Christ, identified with him in his death (Rom 6:3), the church is the cause of universal salvation. In order to bear fruit in all men, the sole condition required of her is to be in union with Christ, to exist in his truth (Jn 15:5). By all that is christian in her, but by this alone, the church is apostolic.

The apostolate is a personal reality

In christianity there are only personal and vital values; there are no others. The apostle is so tied to the existence and life of the church, to her holiness, that the very effects of apostolic action are both immanent to the apostle and salvific for others.

So it is, first of all, for Christ: the salvation of others is achieved in his person; the first and total effect of his merit is his own 'sanctification' (Jn 17:19). He became himself 'wisdom, righteousness and sanctification and redemption' (1 Cor 1:30); he was the first to be born anew (Acts 13:33); he became 'the beginning', became 'head of the body' (Col 1:18), 'life-giving spirit' (1 Cor 15:45), 'the last Adam' (1 Cor 15:45). This last Adam does not propagate himself as our first ancestor did, by infusing life into sources outside himself; men are caught up into *his* death and into the divine action by which he himself is raised; remaining what he is, he becomes the church, he is multiplied by unifying men in himself: he saves them in the depths of his own mystery.

Learning that the pagans wanted to talk with him, Jesus said: 'The hour has come for the Son of man to be glorified. . . . If the grain of wheat dies, it bears much fruit' (Jn 12:23–24). He sees his personal glory in the men who come to him. The image of the grain of wheat does not speak merely of the necessary death, but of the personal glory of Christ, and it tells us that this glory is a proliferation of life.

On the day of the resurrection, the first time St John mentions it, Jesus gives his disciples the name of brothers, of sons of his Father (20:17). A new era is beginning, new relations are set up. Christ becomes what he had not yet been, the disciples are now what they had not hitherto been. Christ is in them and they in him (14:20). He rises as the ear of wheat, heavy with the weight of nations. The evangelist knows that God has glorified Christ himself (17:5), but by making him the Saviour who gathers together in himself the children of God and gives them life. St Paul will say that he is made 'head over all things for the church, which is his body' (Eph 1:22–23). *Considered in Christ, glorification is called resurrection; considered in men, it is called church;* the latter is his body raised in death.

Here we must recall what has already been said: apostolic activity is not a second act in this drama of salvation. It does not presuppose any intervention of God other than that of the glorification of Christ or any activity of Christ other than that of his pasch. God's intervention is *final* plenitude: in his death and his resurrection, Christ is salvation in its total realisation (Col 1:19); nothing is added to it, but God's action in Christ reaches only gradually the limits of men's history, through the church which is created in this action. There is no second act, for the christian reality is not a mere juxtaposition of things, the structure of its mystery is concentric; the church does not succeed to the work of Christ, accomplished once and for all; God's action as it is in Christ, salvation as realised in Christ, is propagated by the church.[1] The body of Christ is given for many; his followers share in this body and are themselves also given for many. The body of Christ is raised for all, and the faithful are 'raised with' him in God's action raising Christ for all.

By this very fact, the church's apostolate will be subject to

[1] We have already seen (above, p. 63) that there is no room for a distinction, in Christ's glorification, between a personal aspect and another which concerns the church; and more than once we shall observe that, in the christian reality, distinctions should not be formulated in terms of disjunction: what is proper to Christ is also proper to the church, at its own level.

*the same law as the redemptive actio.. which is in Christ, since
it is this very action spreading over men: it will be personal.*
External works of themselves will never be salutary for
eternal life, never effective in spreading the gospel. The
apostles' ministry cannot consist in cultic actions in
which they are not personally involved; it is not reduced
to the dispensation of a salvation that someone else—
Christ—has acquired.[1] The church works for the salvation of the world in her own heart, associated with Christ
who has 'consecrated himself'.

After announcing the glorious fruitfulness of his death,
Jesus says to the apostles: 'If anyone serves me, he must
follow me; and where I am, there shall my servant be
also; if any one serves me, the Father will honour him'
(Jn 12:25). The servant of Christ—that is, the apostle—
shares in the Master's destiny. The latter goes to his
death, the servant follows him in death[2] and dwells with
him who, 'lifted up from the earth' on the cross and in
glory, 'will draw all men' to himself (12:32). In this way
the servant will be honoured as Christ himself is honoured: he enters into the mystery of the redemption
which is personal to Christ.

His apostolate will be personal in two ways: in the
part he must provide himself and in the glory with which
the Father will honour him. His part is to follow Christ
in his death, and nothing is so personal to a man as his
death. A few days after inviting his servant to follow

[1] St Paul calls himself 'steward of the mysteries of God' (1
Cor 4:1), but he does not regard himself as being charged
with the distribution of the merits of Christ. For him, the
apostolate is a sharing in the mystery of Christ (1 Cor 4:9–13;
2 Cor 4:10–12).
[2] This is the meaning of 'following Christ' both in St John
(cf. 13:36–38; 21:19, 22) and in the synoptics.

him, Jesus washes the feet of his apostles and requires them to follow his example. He does not exhort them to simple demonstrations of humility and charity, his gesture has a wider import: it announces the purification of the world that he was going to accomplish in the humility of his death. The disciples' ministry will be identical with that of Christ, dsecribed in this gesture; this is how they will have to forgive men's sins, by following Christ in the humble charity of his death: 'I have given you an example, that you also should do as I have done to you. Truly, truly, I say to you, he who is sent is not greater than he who sent him' (Jn 13:15–16). This account bears some resemblance to the synoptic account of the supper at which the apostles share in the body of Christ which is given for many. They will always be apostles through sharing in the body which is given, sent by Christ as he himself is sent (Jn 17:18; 20:21).

In this loyalty in following him, the servant will be honoured like the Son himself (Jn 12:26). Christ is glorified in the fruits of his death: the apostles will be honoured by themselves also bearing fruit. Jesus assures them of this: 'I am the vine, you are the branches. He who abides in me, and I in him, he it is that bears much fruit' (Jn 15:5). The glory of a vine, its unique glory, is to be fruitful. God shares his own glory with his Son and those who are Christ's are in him sons of God, 'fellow heirs' (Rom 8:17) in his glory, in this glory proper to God, of being life and the source of life. The disciples will thus be 'like their master'. Neither above him (Mt 10:24–25), nor beneath him; renouncing themselves even to death and exorbitantly exalted in themselves, bearing in themselves fruits of eternal life, like their God and Father, with Christ in his death and his resurrection: 'As he is, so are we' (1 Jn 4:17).

The immanence of the fruits of the apostolate

How mysterious is the way in which the 'fruits' belong
to the very existence of the apostolate! The disciple is
himself rich with the riches of his apostolate. These latter
are not added to his holiness—neither does the church
add anything to Christ, nor is she herself added to him—
they are in some way immanent to his holiness and its
expression. St Paul thinks that the power of his grace is
adapted to his apostolate: 'His grace toward me was not
in vain. On the contrary, I worked harder than any of
them' (1 Cor 15:10). He knows that he will be judged on
the lasting value of his work, that he is identified himself in God's eyes with the fruits of his labour (1 Cor
3:11–15). The communities born of his apostolate will
be his crown and joy for eternity: 'What is our hope or
joy or crown of boasting before our Lord Jesus at his
coming? Is it not you?' (1 Thess 2:19; Phil 4:1). The
salvation of others will constitute the apostle's own salvation: 'Christ is proclaimed; and in that I rejoice . . .
For I know that this will turn out for my deliverance'
(Phil 1:18–19). Thanks to the salvation of others, 'in the
day of Christ I may be proud that I did not run in vain
or labour in vain' (Phil 2:16). 'I have become all things
to all men, that I might by all means save some. I do it
all for the sake of the gospel, that I may share in its
blessings' (1 Cor 9:22–23). Saint Paul will not have
thrown away his life, 'he will be saved in the salvation
he brought to others.'[1]

[1] A. Sataké, 'Apostolat und Gnade bei Paulus' in *NTS*, 15
(1968), p. 105. Another exegete does not hesitate to write:
according to St Paul, 'no one can have a private claim to

If it is true that all the faithful in this holy and apostolic church are apostles, we must conclude that a christian's success in the evening of life will be measured by the good that he has done to his brothers for eternal life. His harvest for eternity, his 'weight of glory' (2 Cor 4:17), he will find in his brethren who are saved. Is a christian who believes, loves and hopes, so much concerned anyway with the merits of his own works? His desire goes far beyond personal salvation towards these fruits of eternal life, this life of his brethren, this church that he helps to create in Christ for ever.

It seems that the fruits belong to him for ever, they will always be the fruits born of his fidelity. In several parables on the parousia, the faithful servants and labourers, when the master returns, receive as reward a greater ministry that they will exercise for ever. The steward, once at the head of the household servants, finds himself 'set over all his master's possessions' (Mt 24:47). Because he was 'faithful over a little', the servant who made his talents bear fruit will be 'set over much' (Mt 25:21, 23), he will enter into 'an active sharing with Christ in his reign',[1] in this reign which is the eternal salvific dominion of Christ. In the parable of the pounds (Lk 19:12–26), the master on his return gives to the faithful servants authority over the cities of the kingdom,

---

salvation . . . The sole proof of having been a christian lies in the brethren whom we have served' (E. Käsemann, *Exegetische Versuche und Besinnungen*, 1, Göttingen 1960, 296).

St Caesarius of Arles (Sermo 204, 4. *CCL* 104, 821) tells us: 'No man lives for himself alone, as no one dies for himself alone . . . a person will receive the reward of blessed retribution together with and for as many as he has edified by the example of a holy life.'

[1] Note on Matthew 25: 21 in the Jerusalem Bible.

to him who made ten pounds authority over ten cities, to him who made five pounds authority over five cities. Such authority in the eschatological kingdom can only be the authority of grace, an influence for eternal salvation. By his earthly labours, the servant made his talent of grace fruitful: it seemed to be 'a little', but it was God's gift which multiplied and grew great, to become —beyond all earthly appearances—the participation in Christ's salvific royalty for eternity.

All this is difficult to conceive and express. But the wonderful image used by scripture and tradition ought to convince us of the fact that the fruits of his apostolate do belong to the christian in this way: the church is mother of men, and for ever. Like the children of men, those of God are born from the living substance of their mother. But, while human birth separates for ever the children from their mother, the children of God are born by being integrated into the substance and life of the mother and in fact for ever. The day will come when she will no longer be in the pangs of childbirth and yet will remain the mother who is always giving birth, because her children will be in her finally in the fullness of their birth.

Christian feeling, confirmed by the Second Vatican Council, is aware of one christian who has taken on the role of the whole church: the Virgin Mary. That is why she is invoked as mother of the faithful for ever. And since we know that each of the faithful is called to take on the role of the whole church, each one then can share in the privilege of this eternal motherhood.

6

HOLY FOR ALL MEN

The christian can give the life with which he lives; the grace that belongs to him is fruitful in another person. How are these things to be understood? Of course, they cannot be understood and explained. But are the statements at least credible? Are they supported and illuminated by the assured truths of our faith?

I—SALVATION IS THE GIFT OF SELF

The problem of a personal life salutary for others takes shape first of all—as we said—in Christ: the salvation of *his* death and *his* resurrection is inalienably personal to him and yet it is universal. For Christ died to 'the flesh', which closes man up in himself, and was transformed into the Spirit, which is self-communication: he 'became a life-giving spirit' (1 Cor 15:45), a being open to others, given to others, source of life by the very fact of his existence. How inexplicable is this existence of someone who not only gives, but is the gift of himself, good not only at heart but with all that he is. Man on this earth cannot form an idea of this, for he cannot experience it; but he has an intimation and desire of it, from the time when he sets himself to love in truth. Christ can put this loving desire into effect, when he has entered into his filial plenitude and become like his God and Father, who not only loves but is love. In Jesus Christ and through him, love within creation is what it is in God.

St Paul had received a revelation from the Lord, who
is 'made our righteousness and sanctification' (1 Cor
1:30); he felt that he was 'known' by Christ and wanted
'to know' him by sharing his existence and one and the
same destiny (Phil 3:10). The formulas repeated unceasingly of 'Christ in us' and 'us in Christ', of a shared
death and resurrection, as well as the johannine statements about a Christ who dwells and lives in us, all reveal something of the mystery of the Saviour whose existence and redemptive acts are both communal and
personal.

By introducing the church into the communion of his
being and his redemptive acts, Christ raises her to this
open existence, existence as gift of self, which is proper
to him. He submits the church to the test of his own
death in which he is transformed into a 'life-giving
spirit'; she becomes 'one spirit' with him (1 Cor 6:17),
one and the same 'life-giving spirit'. The salvation
brought by Christ is more than forgiveness granted to
the church or a very holy thing deposited in her, more
even than elevation to a divine dignity; salvation is the
transformation of a being closed up in himself into a man
of fellowship and self-giving. Grace liberates men by
making them open; it takes away sin by giving self-
giving; it saves by creating men in the church, in a
community of existence and life among themselves in
Christ. Man when saved is the gift of himself and source
of unity.

On earth, salvation is not yet fully achieved; but from
now on man is 'renewed after the image of his creator'
(Col 3:10), for the Christ to whom he is united has
become 'the new creature', in whom there is no with-
drawal into himself, no self-assertion in unshared pos-

sessions. Without meeting any obstacle, the Spirit imposes on Christ the law of his own being which is sharing and diffusion of himself, and those who belong to Christ live under the same law.

Christ then is not 'consecrated' (Jn 17:19) for himself alone, nor the church for herself alone. They can both say when speaking of all men: 'For their sake I consecrate myself, that they also may be sanctified.' The more intense the holiness of someone, the more personal it is, the less is it reserved to that person alone. Before it becomes a duty, sharing is the law of Christian existence. Grace sanctifies by making men open: its very power to sanctify each individual is that by which it is poured out on others.

II—AT THE HEART OF THE WORLD

In order to be the source, the church must be placed at the point where everything begins, at the centre in order to spread outwards, at the heart in order to flow everywhere. It is not sufficient for her to share in redemptive power, the power she holds must find a fulcrum in order to raise up the world.

Christ 'descended into the lower parts of the earth' and at that very point, without leaving these depths, was raised up above all things in the fullness of God (Eph 4:9): he was placed at the heart of the world and had become the heart of the world. He had announced that his departure would be his final coming: 'I go away and I will come'. His glorification is his parousia for the salvation of all. He makes every man his neighbour, because he has become close to all, in order to bring all things into unity under one head (Eph 1:10).

The church is carried along with her Lord, into these depths which are also 'at the head of all', whence Christ can fill all things (Eph 1:22–23); she is associated with his fullness (Col 2:9), situated with him at the world's centre, and becomes with him the centre of the world's salvation. Her holiness can spread over the world, because the church is holy in Christ; her labours, her prayer, her trials, are for the benefit of the world; she exists in effect for all, since she exists in her Lord.

All mankind has already undergone a baptism in Christ, which is also baptism in the church, a beginning of salvation—admittedly, still inadequate—and a call for fullness. Men are already born and live in a fellowship of grace by the very fact of striving to live in human fellowship. This fellowship has not yet the right to the name of church of Christ and communion of saints, for only those have the right to be so described who already on earth are gathered together in Christ in his death and resurrection. But, surrounding these first fruits that God is given on earth, are wider circles reaching to the ultimate limits of mankind, frontiers circumscribing the external zones of the irradiation of Christ in his church. These wider orbits have Christ also as centre and belong already in some sense to the church, to the communion of saints.[1]

No one knows by what route the grace of the saints comes to these distant human beings. It is by the Spirit that Christ is Lord of salvation, that the church is the body of Christ and mother of men; and the Holy Spirit moves invisibly along invisible ways (cf Jn 3:8).

The early christians had a lively sense of being engaged in an action on a universal scale for the salvation

[1] Cf *The Church*, 13 and 16.

of all men: a certainty that gave them an absolutely irresistible enthusiasm. This is evident in the *Epistle to Diognetus*, written by a christian, probably from Alexandria, to a pagan functionary in order to enlighten the latter about christianity. The author recalls a saying of St Paul and applies it to christians as a whole: 'They are poor and make many rich'[1]; then, with extraordinary boldness, he makes the unheard of claim: 'To put it shortly what the soul is in the body, that the christians are in the world.'[2]

In the philosophy of the period there was talk of a cosmic soul, a divine principle penetrating, 'maintaining' and 'sustaining' the cosmos in the same way that the soul gives life to man's body and this cosmic principle was identified with God himself.[3] And here was a small group of men, lost in the crowd, mocked and persecuted, which claimed this role of universal immanence and cosmic animation: the soul of the world is simply the christian fellowship. 'The soul has been shut up in the body, but itself sustains the body; and christians are confined in the world as in a prison, but themselves sustain the world.'[4] This certainty of their immense responsibility forbade them to fail in their mission: 'God has appointed them to so great a post and it is not right for them to decline it.'[5]

This is a stupendous claim. But the *Epistle to Diognetus* only repeats in the language of Greek philosophy what

[1] *Epistle to Diognetus* v, 13 (Loeb translation).
[2] *Ibid.*, vi, 1. Vatican II quotes this text in *The Church*, 38, and *Church in the Modern World*, 40.
[3] 'What is God? The soul of the universe' (Seneca, *Quaestiones naturales, Praef.* 13).
[4] *Epistle to Diognetus* vi, 7.
[5] *Ibid.*, vi, 10.

is said in the gospel: 'You are the salt of the earth . . .
you are the light of the world. A city set on a hill cannot
be hid' (Mt 5:13–14). The disciples are the salt of the
whole earth, the light of the whole world; they are the
city on the hill, Sion, the promised city, on the highest
of the mountains, to which 'all the nations shall flow'
(Is 2:2–3; Mic 4:1–3; Is 56:6–8). 'This messianic people,
although it . . . may more than once look like a small
flock, is nonetheless a lasting and sure seed of unity,
hope, and salvation for the whole human race. Established by Christ, . . . it is used by him as an instrument
for the redemption of all, and is sent forth into the whole
world as the light of the world and the salt of the earth.'[1]

Only a faith in Jesus Christ, true Son of God, heroic-
ally naive, as Christ requires—'unless you become like
children'—a faith humble enough not to blush when
making claims which—humanly speaking—are absurd,
a faith full of love for her Lord, permits the church to
assume a universal responsibility for salvation. The
church believes that the Lord's body is 'given for the life
of the world' and that she herself has become in the
apostle Peter, in the apostle Paul, and in every one of
her true believers—as an ancient writer puts it—a pure
food of salvation for men.[2]

All her loyalty is involved in this faith and in this
apostolic longing. This is what makes her the Bride:
faith in her Lord, the saviour of the whole world; her
hope, believing in, longing and searching for universal

[1] *The Church*, 9. Cf *Church in the Modern World*, 40: The church
'serves as a leaven and as a kind of soul for human society';
Laity, 2: 'The church . . . brings all men to share in
Christ's saving redemption.'
[2] Origen, *In Levit. hom* 7, 5, *PG* 12, col. 486.

salvation; the charity that unites her to Christ in bringing about this salvation. The church 'is born for nothing else except to propagate everywhere the reign of Christ, so as to bring all men to share in his salutary redemption.'[1] She is the 'universal sacrament of salvation', the 'instrument of the redemption'.[2]

Such is the unique vocation of the church. Salvation is not reserved to christians alone: God creates and sustains all human existence in his saving love and in Christ, dead for all and risen for all. But it is for christians to be gathered together, from the time of this earthly life, in the mystery of Christ to which God calls all men and by which he wishes to effect the salvation of all. In Christ they are a priestly people:[3] they alone, it seems, here on earth.[4] Once Christ was alone in his death for many. Now once more they are alone, Christ and his own, in death for many, the little flock, that of the Lamb who takes away the sin of the world.

This is how the church emerges and can be distinguished. In her the eschatological salvation of Christ's death and resurrection is projected in advance into men's history: it acts on men who are dispersed, draws them effectively and sustains them with the power of the kingdom until they too have attained salvation.

All this is already a reality, but a reality which must

[1] Pius xi, Encyclical *Rerum Ecclesiae, Acta Apostolicae Sedis*, 18 (1926), 65.
[2] *The Church*, 1, 9, 48, 54; *Liturgy*, 5; *Church in the Modern World*, 45; *Missions*, 1, 5.
[3] *The Church*, 10.
[4] We are not denying here what was said above (p. 38), about the salvation initiated in every man and the mutual aid of which non-christians are capable in regard to salvation. But it is in Christ and in the church that there is found the reality of salvation, the source of salvation for all.

be accomplished unceasingly. Baptism is a door open to an infinite, to which entry must not be barred. And, when baptism has been received, it is still necessary to become a christian, to the very end. 'Which of these three, do you think, *became* neighbour to the man who fell among the robbers?' Christ asked (Lk 10:36). By baptism, the christian becomes the universal neighbour for salvation of every man and must never cease to become such. The demands of christianity are without limit, not only because God must be loved in his infinity, but also because of the innumerable human multitude to which the christian is accountable. In face of this enormous task we must never cease to pray to God to come to our aid.

7

THE NEED FOR EVANGELISATION*

God destines every human being to the salvation he has effected in Christ. His plan is not a mere intention; his will is never merely an intention, but effects the project at which it aims. From his own resources man cannot gain this salvation: he has to consent to the divine will to save. From these two truths the certain conclusion emerges that, unless he refuses it, every man will obtain salvation. But it is not sufficient merely to assert this. The ways of universal salvation are obscure. At this level of means the assertion itself seems to be contradicted, for the necessary way—revealed by God—is faith in Jesus Christ and attachment to the church: a faith and attachment that presuppose the apostolic preaching. And yet a large part of mankind will perhaps never hear this message on earth.

Today we are presented with answers to the problem which were once unknown. Careful and sympathetic study has revealed authentic values of the gospel in non-christian religions and among the human beings who practise these, in fact among many supposed atheists. These ideas can have originated only in God, in a divine word spoken in these men's hearts and to which they consent. It is a fact then that God speaks also in the hearts of non-christians, that the church's preaching is not the sole means of evangelisation: for, even to christians, God addresses his word not only through the

* This chapter first appeared in *Spiritus* 32 (1967), 380–395.

church but by means of his whole creation. And again therefore it is a fact that these 'pagans' too are believers, for any consent to the word of God is an act of faith.

In recent centuries the theology of the 'salvation of unbelievers' had reached an impasse. Its concept of faith made belief impossible for a person who had not heard of the gospel. Faith was regarded primarily as an assent to revealed truths, an assent that presupposes the church's preaching or—in default of this—a direct revelation of these truths. Understood in this way, faith is either explicit or does not exist at all; and, since faith is the bond uniting men to the church, a person either belongs to the church by this explicit faith or is in no way linked with the church.

Careful study of scripture has convinced modern theologians that the primary object of faith does not consist in abstract truths, but in a person, God who saves us in Christ; that these truths are secondary in relation to this primary object. In view of this, faith is not simply an assent of the intellect, but the movement of the whole person towards God his Saviour in Christ.

Now the face of the God who saves us in Christ is reflected in a variety of ways in creation, since creation belongs wholly and entirely to the mystery of salvation in Christ (cf Col 1:15-17); it is revealed in every man, for all are created in the image of the Father of Jesus Christ; it is expressed in the great ideals of love and truth, of beauty and justice, and in the events which invite man to surpass himself in accordance with the law of the Event, the Passover event, when Christ went from this world to the Father. By living uprightly, in accordance with the dictates of his heart, man consents to the revelation of the God who saves and—without being

aware of it—he believes, he opens himself to the salvation which is in Christ. St Augustine says: 'The man who
delights in truth, who delights in justice, is drawn by
Christ, for Christ is all this.'[1] In our time, people prefer
to say: 'If a man permits himself to be drawn by truth,
by justice, he is therefore drawn by Christ, for all this is
Christ.' Every upright man, every just man, therefore,
is in some sense christian.

The theology of anonymous christianity

Having established the possibility that every man can
open himself to the grace of Christ without the aid of the
gospel, a number of modern theologians—some very
great names among them—conclude that the man of
good will, even though ignorant of christianity, is a
christian, that his faith is *the* christian faith, that salvation is effected in him, a 'salvation without the gospel'.[2]
This person is given the name of christian, but, since the
fact is not known to the church or to himself, he is called
an 'anonymous christian.' The sole difference which distinguishes this christianity from any other lies—they say
—in its anonymity. Of course the faith of these christians
is imperfect, but only in its formulation: it is a 'sub-
conscious faith' that will have to find its appropriate
formulation at the conscious level; nevertheless, it is
already genuine christian faith. One passes from anonymous christianity to explicit christianity by becoming
conscious of it.

[1] *In Joh. tract.* 26, 4. *CCL* 36, 261.
[2] This is the title of a book by H. Nys, *Salut sans l'Evangile*,
Paris 1966. The author there adopts the standpoint of contemporary theological study on 'the salvation of unbelievers'.
We shall follow this work in our exposition of the theory of
anonymous christianity.

'The task of missions and missionaries therefore is not to bring grace to those who do not yet possess it,' for 'grace is already offered to all'; it does not consist in 'bringing them faith properly so called', for they possess it already, but in 'giving an authentic expression to this faith,' in 'leading this dormant and latent christianity to full christian awareness.' Neither faith nor salvation are dependent on the church's help; saving action precedes the church's action; man is already saved.[1] The church's proper task is to 'make man come to himself', to tell these anonymous ones their name.[2]

Those who have not yet heard the gospel include, not only 'anonymous christians', but also some who, up to the present, 'have refused to give their life for the good of others and of the world'. These are the only real unbelievers and the only non-christians. By the testimony of her faith and especially of her charity, the church will try to shake their egoism and invite them to take up 'a different attitude, oriented to an end that surpasses immediate interests' and will help them to receive the salvation that had already been offered to them.[3]

Two stages

In the process described above there are two stages which must be clearly distinguished. We first saw redemptive

---

[1] H. Nys, 265–269.
[2] Cf Karl Rahner, *Theological Investigations* VI, London and Baltimore, Md, 1969, 390–98. Scripture too says that the convert receives a name, but this is more than a new awareness. The 'new name' expresses a new existence, that of Christ (Rev 2:17; 3:12).
[3] H. Nys, 267–268. This again is not reserved to the church: 'encounters with other men or contacts with secular or religious institutions may have the same result' (p. 268 note).

grace at work in every man, reaching him in advance of
any preaching, rousing in him a commitment of faith
and ordering him towards salvation. At this first stage
theological reflection kept close to scripture and based
itself on the fact of the universal saving will, the unity
of the work of creation and salvation, on faith understood as man's commitment and self-surpassing in regard to the God who saves. Anyone who believes in
redeeming love and looks at the world with sympathy
will accept without more ado these first conclusions.

At a second stage, without bringing in any fresh argu-
ments, but relying solely—it seems—on those which led
to the conclusions already stated, it is asserted that this
faith is *the* christian faith, that these men *are* christians,
and that the church's sole function is to make them aware
of their identity. At this point we begin to hesitate, to
ask if these conclusions are not an extrapolation; to ask
whether, in its final steps, this theological investigation
has made an effort to submit to the necessary[1] light of
scripture.[2]

[1] Even though the problematic is modern, we must look to
scripture for the theology of salvation, since salvation is part
of the mystery of God himself. It is true that the Lord reveals
himself also to believers today in their present problems. But
he does so in terms of the primary and unique revelation.
Contemporary theology can mark out circles wider than its
scriptural basis, but it would be unfaithful to its law, would
no longer be a theology, if it did not develop these circles out
of the first circle, formed at the origin around the point of
the Word's descent into history.
[2] It has often been pointed out that scripture seems to count
for very little in the theory of anonymous christianity. The
starting point of reflection is found in 'various fundamental
data of the traditional theology of the Schools . . . and the
real situation of mankind, of Christianity and of the Church
today' (Karl Rahner, *Theological Investigations*, vi, London

We may take it for granted that every man of good will belongs to the order of salvation, but we would like to *inquire from scripture* about the point on which it was not consulted at all or scarcely consulted, whether the man of good will who does not know Christ is a christian by the mere fact of this good will and lacks only the name of christian.

St Paul, a christian before his conversion?

As a grown man when God 'was pleased to reveal his Son' in him (Gal 1:16),[1] St Paul abandoned a religious situation which more than any other might justifiably be called 'anonymous christianity' and committed himself to Christ. Did he regard his conversion simply as a new awareness of what he was?

All the conditions necessary for an anonymous christian are verified in the case of Paul, the Jew: on God's part, implicit christian evangelisation; on Paul's part, this extraordinary zeal of which he himself was aware (Phil 3:4-6); not to mention the ecclesial structure into which the Jews were integrated.

God had evangelised the believers of the Old Testament intensely, had made them his people, the *ekklesia* which the pagans were to join (Eph 2:11-13). He evangelised less by proclaiming christian truths—al-

---

1969, 397). When scriptural proofs are used, they appear to be invalid (cf H. Kruse, 'Die anonymen Christen exegetisch gesehen' in *Münchener theologische Zeitschrift*, 18 (1967), 2-29).

[1] This text does not mean that God made St Paul aware of a presence of Christ which he already possessed, but that God revealed Christ to him in the depths of his heart, or—more simply—God 'revealed Christ to him'. Cf J. Dupont, *Gnosis*, Louvain 1949, 198.

though these truths are found in outline there—than by bringing the people to share in the realities to come: 'They are Israelites, and to them belong the sonship, the glory, the covenants, the giving of the law, the worship, and the promises; to them belong the patriarchs, and of their race, according to the flesh, is the Christ' (Rom 9:4-5). Israel struck firm roots in its future. The very basis of christianity, the Christ of God by whom a whole people lives, was itself a privilege of Israel. According to Galatians 3:16, in himself alone he constituted the innumerable descendants promised to Abraham (Gen 12:7), signifying that all descent from Abraham was summed up in him, was in some way christian: already Isaac, the son of promise, was not 'born according to the flesh' (Gal 4:23). Thus Christ preceded his own coming. 'Remember that you were at that time separated from Christ, alienated from the commonwealth of Israel' cries the apostle to the ancient pagans (Eph 2:12); he assumes that Israel was not 'separated from Christ'.

St Paul therefore was not unfaithful to his past: it was only by becoming a christian that he remained faithful. It has often been observed that, in his eyes, the Damascus event was not so much a conversion as a vocation, not so much a renunciation as a realisation. He believed that the christian community was the true 'Israel of God' (Gal 6:16). Here then we have the ideal subject to whom the question can be put: *Did the christian revelation bring grace or was it merely a new awareness?* Did it bring faith or simply provide a formulation for a pre-existent faith? Did it only 'lead this man to himself' or was this interiorisation at the same time in fact a total self-surpassing?

If christian revelation were merely this new awareness, the theory of anonymous christianity would find a striking justification in one of the greatest 'converts'; it would be justified at least in regard to judaism, justified to a certain extent in regard to the pagan religions, for in spite of the distance separating them mosaic religion and the pagan religions were not without affinities: twice at least (Gal 4:9; Col 2:8) the apostle places both on the level of the 'weak elemental spirits of the universe'. On the other hand, if the apostle claims that his 'conversion' brought him substantial riches, a totally new reality, then the theology of anonymous christianity is contradicted at the very point at which it should gain the clearest support from scripture.

A wholly new reality

The conversion of St Paul was an illumination: 'scales fell from his eyes'. He saw that he had been caught up from the beginning in the mystery of Christ, 'set apart before being born' (Gal 1:15). In the light of the face of Christ (2 Cor 4:6), he discovered a christian presence throughout the history and literature of Israel. He speaks from experience when he says that the Jew wears a veil over his face when he reads the Old Testament, but that, 'when a man turns to the Lord the veil is removed' (2 Cor 3:16). There is no doubt that 'conversion' for St Paul implied a new awareness of a reality already existing. Nevertheless, this awareness was a secondary—absolutely secondary—phenomenon, produced by the irruption into the apostle's existence of a wholly new reality: the Christ of glory.

'Newness' is a basic category of pauline thought, in every description of christianity: God has introduced 'the new covenant' (1 Cor 11:25; 2 Cor 3:6), that of 'the new life of the Spirit' (Rom 7:6; 2 Cor 3:6); the baptised

are 'a new creation' (2 Cor 5:14–17; Gal 6:15); they
live in 'newness of life' (Rom 6:4): they form together
with Christ a 'new man', 'created after the likeness of
God in true righteousness' (Eph 2:15; 4:24); they are 'a
new lump' (1 Cor 5:7), for they are *born* 'by regeneration
and renewal in the Holy Spirit' (Tit 3:5).

This newness is not merely the emergence of sub-
conscious reality. What is new is not merely knowledge,
but the reality itself, radiant with a light in which the
former realities appear dead and decayed (Rom 7:6),
tied to the past and therefore surpassed (cf Heb 8:13),
an 'old leaven' that is rejected (1 Cor 5:7). For St Paul,
the newness of view is the effect of the transformation he
has suffered. It is not the vision alone, but his eyes that
have been renewed: 'From now on we regard no one
from a human point of view. . . . The old has passed
away, behold, the new has come' (2 Cor 5:16–17; cf Col
3:9–11).

The new christian reality is so original that it recalls
the creation of the first man. The opposition between
the old man and the new is a confrontation between the
two 'Adams', the one created 'a living being'—carnal
existence, possessed of earthly life—and the other who
'became a life-giving spirit', according to God's mode of
existence, which henceforward we must come to resemble
(1 Cor 15:45–49). Each of these two modes of existence
has its origin in a creative action.

The passage from death and decay to newness is constantly linked with faith and baptism (Rom 6:4–6; 7:4–
6; Gal 3:27–28; Col 2:11–15). Something then is hap-
pening, according to St Paul, in this 'explicit' faith and
this baptism, something that belongs to the order of
creation. It is then that God takes possession of men and

makes them what they had not yet been, 'the new nature' (Col 3:10), for God then clothes them with the Lord Jesus (Gal 3:27).

It is true that christianity enabled the apostle to get the true measure of Judaism and to recognise what had always been his own vocation. But St Paul was not placed before his own image that he had never yet seen: it is Christ who has been revealed, and revealed as *the term*, always at work in the Old Testament but transcending it, whom the Jews must come in contact with in a total self-surpassing.

This reality is eschatological

What is essentially new, created by God in the church, is Christ. The first christians were convinced that Christ in his death and resurrection is the *eschaton* of the world: the final reality in which God 'fulfilled' all the promises and all things (cf Acts 13:32f.), the irruption of the kingdom of heaven among men. They knew by faith and the sacraments that they were incorporated in this Christ. The Epistle to the Hebrews asserts with extraordinary vigour the difference between the plane of Christ's activity and that which preceded it. The distance between the two is that between heaven and earth,[1] that which separates the final reality—eternal fullness, 'consummation' of man in God—from its earthly anticipations: an infinite distance. Such a reality is not simply new, it is brand-new, always at its beginning: it is Christ in his resurrection, in the today—forever actual—of his birth in glory (Acts 13:33; Rom 1:4); it is fullness, it is eschatological and therefore has no becoming and no

[1] This is a basic idea, present everywhere in the Epistle to the Hebrews.

morrow. When this total newness enters into history whatever is not part of it appears old, old by its very nature. Every earthly event, as soon as it occurs, belongs to the past; but the eschatological reality which penetrates into the world remains utterly new forever, since it is for ever the future of this world.

A radical difference between time before and after Christ

This new reality entered the world at a precise moment in history: at the 'Hour' of Christ, when he died and was glorified. 'The fullness of time' has a date. For St Paul it is not a matter of indifference whether we live before or after the death of Christ:[1] before that date, man is tied to the old; after it, he can share in the new reality. Of himself and of christians before faith, St Paul says, 'while we were living in the flesh' (Rom 7:5); he sees all Israel as in servitude before 'the time had fully come' (Gal 4:1–4).

Salvation is achieved through death, in the glory of Christ; apart from some limited effects, *it does not go back through the course of history* before the death of Christ (the term of history, by definition, cannot be at the dawn of history).[2] It is not present in its reality at the time of Abraham; even in Christ's earthly life it was not yet

[1] Among others, Oscar Cullmann, *Christ and Time*, London 1951, has shown clearly that salvation is rooted in time.
[2] It seems to me that the theory of anonymous christianity does not take sufficient account of this eschatological character, essential to the salvation which is in Christ. Of course it can be said that a person accepts revelation when he accepts himself, when he fulfils his duties of every day (cf Karl Rahner, *Theological Investigations*, VI, 394). But there is no question in that case either of eschatological revelation or of eschatological salvation. And the specifically christian factor is the eschatological.

present to men: at this time the kingdom was 'near'.

In his earthly existence as such, Christ himself had not yet entered into the kingdom. He had led an existence according to the flesh and, in this respect, belonged to the people of the Old Testament. From the time of his death, he lives according to the Spirit (Rom 1:4; 1 Cor 15:45); from then onwards he is 'saved from death', 'made perfect' (Heb 5:7–9) 'by the glory of the Father' (Rom 6:4) and made 'our righteousness and redemption' (1 Cor 1:30). Final salvation is effected in the once 'carnal' existence of Christ. This difference between two successive modes of being of Christ and the union of the church with Christ to the point of being his body in death and resurrection, it would seem, constitutes a decisive argument against reducing the religious situation before and after the death of Christ to the same level.

Salvation comes to men when Christ comes to them in this often announced coming and of which he said before his death: 'From *now* you will see the Son of man coming' (Mt 26:64). Exegetes have often drawn attention to the importance of this 'now' in primitive theology. 'Once you were darkness, but now you are light in the Lord' (Eph 5:8). 'Now is the day of salvation' (2 Cor 6:2). 'Now the righteousness of God has been manifested[1] . . . It was to prove at the present time . . . that he justifies him who has faith in Jesus' (Rom 3:21, 26). This 'now' signifies that salvation, which appeared in the resurrection of Christ, had not yet reached men before the death of Christ.[2]

[1] The verb is in the perfect tense, this manifestation of justice therefore depends on a definite fact of the past: the death of Christ.

[2] Hebrews 10:19–20 says likewise that we 'enter the sanctuary . . . by the new and living way which he opened for us

Nevertheless, the mere fact of living after Christ's time does not bring a person into this 'now': for Christ's day is nothing but Christ himself in the paschal salvation which comes in history. To belong to his day, we have to meet Christ in history and be 'clothed' with him. That is *why many of our contemporaries belong to the time before Christ* or, to use scriptural language, for them Christ has not yet come. Now it is only in the church that Christ is risen *in* this world, she alone is his real presence in history, since she is his body, his presence and his manifestation. The church's mission is to be the sacrament of Christ, of his coming, of his contact and his action. In her men can *attain* to 'the fullness of time'; outside her, those who are upright in heart are in the same state as the just of the Old Testament: on the way.

The just of the Old Testament and the gift of the Spirit

Does this mean that the Old Testament believers were not sanctified by the grace of the redemption? Certainly they were: Abraham was justified (Rom 4:3); the ancients were righteous (Heb 11:3), saints according to Matthew 27:52. They had faith and were thereby justified (Rom 4:9–12). But the problem is this: was their grace that of Christ in his church, united to him by faith and the sacraments?

In the light of a juridical conception of the redemption, western theology generally asserted, without any

---

through the curtain, that is, through his flesh.' Here again we find the assertion that fellowship in salvation is brought about beginning with a particular individual and from a definite point in history; that the ancients 'did not receive what was promised, . . . that apart from us they should not be made perfect' (Heb 11:39–40).

hesitation, that the grace of the just in the Old Testament was identical with that of the New. If grace was acquired as a sort of commodity, for which Christ paid the price, it can be distributed by God before the death of Christ just as well as after it, both inside and outside the church. If however grace is understood as a gift of the Spirit to man (Rom 5:5) in Christ and in his body, the church, as divine sonship with Christ in his body, the church, then the problem of the identity of grace in the Old and New Testaments immediately arises. The earliest theologians, especially in the East, were either reluctant to consider grace given to the just in the Old Testament as the same or they denied it altogether.[1]

There is firm support in scripture for this denial. From the time of the exile, the outpouring of the Spirit had been *promised* as something characteristic of the last days. The New Testament is even more firm in showing the Spirit to be the eschatological gift made to men in Jesus Christ (Gal 3:14). According to St Paul, this gift was not granted before the death of Christ. The latter had first led an existence 'according to the flesh,' then was made alive in the Spirit (Rom 1:4; cf. 1 Pet 3:18), 'vindicated' in the holiness of the Spirit (1 Tim 3:16), transformed into a life-giving spirit (1 Cor 15:45), and thus became the source of the Holy Spirit. Formerly promised, now available to men (Gal 3:14), this gift is christic and ecclesial, the privilege of Christ and of the church united, by faith and sacrament, to his body made alive in the Spirit (1 Cor 6:17; Eph 4:4).[2]

[1] Cf. G. Philips, 'La grâce des justes de l'Ancien Testament' in *Eph. Theol. Lov.* 23 (1947), 521–556; 24 (1948), 23–58. P. Grelot, *Le sens chrétien de l'Ancien Testament*, Paris 1962, 159–164.
[2] Cf Irenaeus, *Adv. Haer.* III, 24, 1.

The assertion of the fourth gospel is categorical: 'The Spirit had not been given, because Jesus was not yet glorified' (Jn 7:39); Jesus has to 'ascend' by way of the cross into the glory of the Father in order to give the Spirit (16:7), and then he will send him from the Father (15:26; cf. 14:26), believers can then drink at the rivers that flow from his side (7:37–39).

Certainly the just of the Old Testament also experienced themselves the sanctifying intervention of the Holy Spirit (cf Ps 51:11–14). But if the gift of the Spirit in the New Testament is tied to the bodily glorification of Christ, if it is available to men only after the death of Christ, there must be a qualitative difference[1] between the grace of the Old Testament and this gift of the Spirit; *the paschal gift made in Christ, and in his body the church, cannot be assimilated merely to a new awareness of a reality already present.* To deny the newness of this gift would be to deny first and foremost the reality of Christ's glorification and the profound difference between Christ's existence according to the flesh and his existence according to the Spirit.

Since the grace of the Spirit is different, so too is *the sonship* that Israel enjoyed (Rom 9:4):

'An heir, even if he has actually inherited everything, is no different from a slave for as long as he remains a child. He is under the control of guardians and administrators until he reaches the age fixed by his father. Now before we came of age we were as good

---

[1] Older authors too were aware of this scriptural problem and tried to define the nature of grace in the Old Testament. Petau's opinion that grace in the Old Testament was given as a force is not without firm biblical support. Petavius, *Dogmata Theologica*, Ed. Vives 1865, III, 493.

as slaves to the elemental principles of this world, but when the appointed time came, God sent his Son, born of a woman, born a subject of the Law, to redeem the subjects of the Law and to enable us to be adopted as sons. The proof that you are sons is that God has sent the Spirit of his Son into our hearts: the Spirit that cries, "Abba, Father", and it is this that makes you a son, you are not a slave any more; and if God has made you son, then he has made you heir' [Gal 4:1-7 Jerusalem Bible translation].

In the first verses the apostle does not assert that the Old Testament believer was already son and legitimate heir.[1] The infancy in question is not divine infancy,[2] but the situation of mankind not yet come of age; men become children of God, enter into their heritage and into liberty, when the fullness of time comes for them. Previously they had not been sons, but slaves (v.7), subjects

---

[1] These two verses provide a basis for comparison. In order to understand what is the exact truth proposed, the meeting point between the image and the truth has to be defined. This point is slavery and the entry into freedom. Cf Bertram, *TWNT*, VI, 920. A child is freed from his tutors and enters into his inheritance only when he comes of age. Mankind likewise, destined for the freedom of sonship, had to wait for the fullness of time. The comparison does not permit us to assert that men had previously already possessed this sonship and the right to the inheritance. This is denied anyway in what follows (vv.5, 7).

[2] St Paul generally uses the word 'child' in a pejorative sense. Here, paradoxically, infancy means the time of ageing, before coming to birth as sons. To say that, according to Romans 9:4, Israel already possessed this sonship, would be to forget 'that there is an abyss between the adoptive sonship of the New Testament and the theocratic sonship of the Old' (F. Prat, *La Théologie de Saint Paul*, II, Paris 1923[6], pp. 386-387).

of the law (v.5), subject to 'elemental principles that can do nothing and give nothing' (vv.3, 9). They did not receive what was promised, since . . . 'they were not to reach perfection except with us' (Heb 11:40). What is lacking is not a new awareness, but the reality itself: 'They all died, not having received what was promised, but having seen it and greeted it from afar' (Heb 11:13).

Can the reality of salvation precede its revelation?
To prove that God now makes us his sons, St Paul appeals to christian experience: 'Because you are sons, God has sent the Spirit of his Son into our hearts, crying, "Abba! Father!"' (Gal 4:6). The gift of grace and the revelation of grace here go together. Are they not always together and necessarily so?[1] Salvation is not something super-added, but man himself as realised in God. How could salvation remain unknown, since self-awareness characterises man in his perfection. Salvation is man's achievement at his peak, at the point where he is a person, in his relations with someone else: at the peak of his personal relations, where he says in Jesus Christ, 'Abba! Father!'. Do genuine personal relations exist when the other person is not known?

Whatever we may think of all this, God's covenant with his people—the new, especially—does not merely imply, it is, a mutual knowledge (Jer 31:31–34), and the pagans are those 'who do not know God' (cf 1 Thess 4:5).

For God's gift is light. According to St Paul, man is

[1] H. de Lubac said this already in a very fine book which can still provide inspiration today: 'To sum up, revelation and redemption are bound up together' (*Catholicism*, London 1950, 113). In *Paradoxe et mystère de l'Eglise* (Paris 1967, 160), he quotes Teilhard de Chardin: 'Revelation creates spirits by the very fact of enlightening them.'

renewed in knowledge: 'You have put on the new
nature, which is being renewed in knowledge after the
image of its creator' (Col 3:10). According to St John,
Christ is personally light coming into this world; all
grace is luminous: 'You know him, for he dwells in you'
(14:17); 'a little while, and the world will see me no
more, but you will see me; because I live, you will live
also' (14:19). This is how Jesus knows his Father (10:15)
who dwells in him (14:11).

Then again, *the light that comes constitutes the gift of grace.*
The economy of salvation is 'a secret and hidden wisdom
of God' which is realised in us (1 Cor 2:7; Rom 16:25–
26; Eph 3:9–12; Col 1:26–28). The divine light takes
possession of man: 'Now that you have come to know
God, or rather to be known by God' (Gal 4:9; Col 1:13).
The light of the face of Christ, its source, is shed on man
and transforms him (2 Cor 3:18; 4:6). All this takes
place now, 'for once you were darkness, but now you are
light' (Eph 5:8).

Could this light of grace have existed in the Old
Testament, the very same reality and yet obscure? Must
we not conclude that *the progress of revelation is identical
with the realisation of salvation*? In the Old Testament
God did not make known his trinitarian mystery: was
this perhaps because he had not yet made himself accessible to men? Man in the mystery of the Trinity—man in
his fullness, from the time of the glorifying death—is the
man Jesus; the rest enter into fullness after him and his
glorifying death. Jesus said: 'We will come to him and
make our home with him' (Jn 14:23). This indwelling
was a future reality: the community will know it and
enjoy it 'in that day' (14:20, 23).

In the Old Testament the Spirit is manifested as a

divine force, like a powerful wind,[1] and not as God's love in man's heart (Rom 5:5). But he is already promised under a new image (cf. Is, Jer, Ezek), that of living water which—as Jesus says—*will* become a spring welling up to eternal life in the very heart of the believer (Jn 4:14; 7:37–39). Does this not mean that for men the Spirit was at first a force, creative and of course sanctifying, but that the presence of the Spirit itself, God's immanence to man and principle of divine life, was reserved for the day of Christ?

The law of the Old Testament was imposed from outside, promulgated from the heights of Sinai. But in Jeremiah 31:33 God promises a new order in which 'I will put my law within them, and I will write it upon their hearts'. Does this not mean that the moral law of the Old Testament was not yet an immanent law, was not yet the Holy Spirit in person in the hearts of the faithful, which constitutes the law of the New Testament?[2] From the Old Testament to the New, *progress is always from a transcendence which brings salvation from outside to an immanence where God becomes salvation.* From then onwards there is a man who claims for himself the name that Yahweh had adopted when he revealed himself as the saviour of Israel (Ex 3:14): 'I AM' (Jn 8:58). But this saving '*I Am*' does not send his aid (cf Ex 3:14), he is himself the salvation that is given: '*I Am* the bread of life', man possesses him who *is* salvation (Jn 6:54, 56). From now on God is within man. The progress of revelation comes about through divine incarnation.

[1] Cf P. van Imschoot, 'L'Esprit de Yahvé, principe de vie morale dans l'Ancien Testament' in *Eph. Theol. Lov.*, 16 (1939), 467.
[2] *Lex nova quae est ipse Spiritus Sanctus* (St Thomas Aquinas, *In Rom.* 8, lect. 1; cf *Summa Theologica* I–II, q. 106 a. 1).

Revelation and salvation develop therefore in one and the same movement; revelation itself creates the mutual fellowship of God and man, the covenant both of the Old and of the New Testament; for revelation is the very action of God by which he unveils himself, comes to us, gives himself to us, right up to the supreme revelation which is also supreme donation, when he begets Christ for us, raising him up in his death (Acts 13:33).[1] Revelation is itself covenant from the time that it is accepted by man, a 1 it is revelation which stimulates the acceptance of faith and reaches there its consummation.

There are, however, many still today who belong to the time before Jesus Christ, before the final revelation of God in Jesus Christ within history. The church's mission is to bring them the gospel, so that salvation is effected in men simultaneously with its revelation.

Creative evangelisation

The scriptural meaning of 'the gospel' is a message effective of salvation; as St Paul puts it: 'The gospel is the power of God for salvation to every one who has faith' (Rom 1:16).[2] What scripture says is so clear that there is no need to demonstrate it again after so many others have done so: preaching is 'the word at work' (1 Thess 2:13), revealing and operating simultaneously. The gos-

[1] *Revelation*, 2: 'God speaks to men . . . so that he may invite and take them into fellowship with himself.' Cf 1 Jn 1:2-3. On this subject see also the simple and profound study by G. Moran, *Theology of Revelation*, London, 1966.
[2] If St Paul adds immediately, 'in it (the gospel) the righteousness of God is revealed', this righteousness is revealed by making man righteous (Rom 3:26) and not merely by making him aware of a righteousness already possessed.

pel is made known, summons man and is communicated;
to receive the word is to be saved (Rom 10:5–10); the
apostles are fellow workers of the God who saves (1 Cor
3:9), stewards of his mysteries (1 Cor 4:1); they even
form part of the mystery of salvation which is diffused
over the world; they are a 'fragrance' from Christ, 'from
life to life' (2 Cor 2:14–16), a saving presence of Christ
dead and risen (2 Cor 4:5–12). They are *makers, not
revealers of Christians*: 'I became your father in Christ
Jesus through the gospel' (1 Cor 4:15), 'until Christ be
formed in you' (Gal 4:19). The apostle thinks that anyone who opposes his preaching to the pagans is prevent-
ing their salvation (1 Thess 2:16).[1] To say that the
church's mission is 'not to bring grace' but to confirm
its presence is to speak a language alien to scripture.[2]

Faith through the gospel: a threshold to be crossed

Faith is the first effect of this evangelisation, it is the
acceptance of the proffered salvation. Abraham 'believed God' (Rom 4:3): his was true faith, authentic
adherence to God who saves. But if Abraham's faith
resembles that of the christian in its structure, its *object*
is different. Abraham believes in God who wishes to

[1] By speaking in this way we have no intention of retracting
what was said above on p. 36.
[2] The Fathers kept to the line of scriptural thought. Analys-
ing and summing up what they said, K. Delahaye, *Ecclesia
Mater*, writes: 'In the thought of the primitive Fathers, the
promise of the Word of God is already salvation itself, the
beginning and substance of salvation' (p. 221). 'For him
(Irenaeus) the event of Christ is above all revelation of God,
and salvation is therefore revealed truth, . . . preaching is
an active propagation of life, . . . a realisation of salvation'
(pp 222–223). 'For him (Hippolytus) the announcement of
salvation is not merely a preliminary to salvation, but it is

raise descendants for him, Paul believes in God who divinely begets Jesus Christ for us, by raising him from the dead (Acts 13:33; Rom 1:4). The salvation effected however is to be judged, not by the psychological structure of faith, but in the light of what God offers, in the light of the object which is God's creative word—Jesus Christ himself whom God raises for us—and to which man consents in faith. God's intervention on Abraham's behalf is one thing, the raising of Jesus Christ for the world's salvation, to which Paul gives his faith, is another.

The *effect* of this faith too will be different. Abraham becomes just and the father of a great people; the apostle submits in faith to God's action in raising Christ, he enters with Christ into the fellowship of death to the flesh and of eternal life (Col 2:12; Phil 3:8–10). One is perpetuated in his race, the other in fellowship in the resurrection of Christ. As to the justice from which both benefit, the same word covers different realities in the light of the context of Old or New Testament.[1] After having praised the faith of Abraham and the ancients, the Epistle to the Hebrews recognises that they 'did not receive what was promised' (11:39).

---

this salvation in its very essence' (p. 224). Likewise, for Clement of Alexandria and Origen, 'knowledge of the truth is already the achievement of salvation' (p. 227). To sum up: 'In the earliest documents, the church is above all mediatrix of truth and thereby of life' (p. 254). Is it necessary to define more exactly that the knowledge of which these Fathers are speaking is not simple apprehension by the mind?

[1] The Old Testament had said: 'The righteous shall live by his faith' (Hab 2:4), promising at the time of the Chaldaean invasions that the man who put his faith in God would endure. For St Paul this text means that adherence to God in Christ gives the righteousness of eternal life.

Although in the structure of the act there is an analogy between christian faith and any other commitment to God (or an image of God), this christian faith is still distinct also by its *structure*. God demands this faith for someone in whom he saves the world: 'We have believed in Christ Jesus' (Gal 2:16). Man opens himself to this other person through faith, and opens himself to him as to his total salvation, dedicating himself to this Lord for eternity in submission (2 Cor 10:5; Phil 2:10–11; Jn 20:28) and in friendship (cf Gal 2:16, 19–20). Like all friendship, this faith is unique because of the personal uniqueness of the friend; and here the uniqueness is transcendent in virtue of Christ's fullness of being and of the salvation that is in him. Such a faith cannot exist without knowledge. Is there friendship without mutual knowledge? It is in fact by 'knowing' the Bridegroom in one single body that the church is the bride giving her faith. And knowledge in turn presupposes evangelisation. St Paul insists on this in Rom 10:14–17.[1]

If the Jews, with their 'zeal for God' (Rom 10:2), could reject the gospel and become 'unbelievers' (2 Cor

---

[1] In the light of salvation history, it does not seem logical to say that 'implicit', 'concealed' or 'disguised faith' already constitutes *the* christian faith. In an evolutionary view of the world, the appearance of a new species is not regarded as the manifestation of a being existing already, hidden, in the preceding species; evolution is thought to be, in some sense, creative. In salvation history what is new is not the revelation of a salvation already old, but the divine realisation of salvation itself starting out from the realities that prepared it. P.-A. Liégé thinks it would be better not to speak of implicit faith in the sense given to the term in the theory of anonymous christianity, but to speak simply of 'men of good will' ('La foi implicite en procès' in *Parole et Mission* 41 (1968), 210–213).

4:4), faced with God raising Christ, if they 'did not submit to God's righteousness' (Rom 10:3), it is because there was a threshold to cross from their Old Testament faith to that of Christ.

This threshold is the death of Christ

Jesus had said that his disciple, the believer, would follow him to death (Mt 16:24); St Paul had experienced through faith fellowship with Christ in death (Phil 3:10); every adult christian at some time perceives that faith has installed him uncomfortably high above the earth, with Christ on the cross. An upright man would have the strength to be honest; he might even be capable of giving his life for a just cause. It is a different thing to believe that God sends his own Son and raises him for us with infinite power for our salvation. Who could really believe this without the aid of this same power of God? However harsh the experience may be, according to St Paul, it is certain that faith makes man live with the very life of Christ ('you were raised with him—Christ—through faith'), in a fellowship in his death, 'by putting off the body of flesh' (Col 2:11–12; Gal 2:19–20). Faith is part of the newness of the kingdom that God creates at the end, in Jesus Christ.

In St John, Jesus promises that he will draw all things to himself on the cross and in glory (12:32), but he says of his follower: 'Where I am—on the cross and in glory —there shall my servant be also' (12:26). *Is not this where the difference lies, between being on the way towards Christ and being in Christ?* All are drawn towards him, but the servant is already with him, in his mystery of redemption: 'He is the source of your life in Christ Jesus' (1 Cor 1:30).

The road and its term

St Paul and the Epistle to the Hebrews provide us with two very definite facts: Israel was the chosen people, but had not yet reached the end of its road. The time of 'perfection' is reached in Christ, in his death under Pontius Pilate; Christ is the eschatological kingdom in which we are inscribed henceforward through faith. Through faith, christians already reach the end of time (1 Cor 10:11); they belong to the day (1 Thess 5:8). Undoubtedly, they too are still on the way (cf 1 Cor 10:1–11), but *towards a salvation that they possess*; the parousia is already realised for them, as it was promised (Jn 14:18–21), and the eucharist is the proof of this; they are the body and, *through their own head*, they emerge in the age to come: 'He made us sit with him in the heavenly places' (Eph 2:6).[1]

Having been promised salvation, Israel possessed it up to a point, for the divine promise is also the beginning of its realisation. But none of these means for starting out could make them christians, since they were only the shadow of the body (Col 2:17; Heb 10:1), the prophecy of the final reality.[2] The manna was 'spiritual' and the rock too (1 Cor 10:3–4). But this spiritual element was

[1] The christian too is still on the way: he must put on Christ (Rom 13:14), but a Christ he has already put on by faith and baptism (Gal 3:27). The eucharist shows us how he goes towards the Christ he already possesses, but in the imperfection of earthly time, towards a kingdom of which he is already a citizen (Phil 3:20). The situation of the unbeliever in face of eschatological reality is different: he is not capable of sharing the eucharist, the meal in a kingdom of which he is not yet part.

[2] A theology which stands for the identity of grace in the Old Testament and the New introduces into the Old Testament a parallelism, on the one hand, of means of salvation

a token, inferior to later reality. In St John, Jesus says: 'Your fathers ate the manna in the wilderness, and they died' (6:49); in order to live eternally, a manna is needed which is the body of Christ, given in the church.

The means offered in the Old Testament had their own consistency; although dependent on the body, the shadow is not the body. The kingdom was not only at the end of the road, it was also above it; when it comes, its incidence is vertical, the divine intervention is creative: God divinely begets his Son for us, raising him in death. Eschatology achieves everything in a total self-transcendence, it is the fullness of *creation*.

Before St Paul had entered into the kingdom (Col 1:13), 'there was a man sent from God'. Among all the men of the Old Testament, none was greater than John the Baptist. But in his lifetime the kingdom had not yet been inaugurated. In his day, John may well have been very holy and the greatest of saints, but 'he who is least in the kingdom of heaven is greater than he' (Mt 11:11). For the kingdom is greater than all that precedes it.[1]

---

incapable (cf Hebrews) of giving grace in the christian sense and, on the other, of a hidden action of God giving precisely this grace.

[1] The commentary of Cyril of Alexandria on this saying is well known: 'In the holy prophets there shone the living splendour of a light of the Spirit capable of leading to the knowledge of things to come, . . . but we are assured that not only does this guiding light dwell in those who believe in Christ, but the Spirit himself dwells there and is their guest. That is why we are rightly called temples of God, although none of the holy prophets was called a temple of God. If this is not so, how can we interpret the words: "Truly, I say to you, among those born of women there has risen no one greater than John the Baptist; yet he who is least in the kingdom of heaven is greater than he"? What is this king-

And it pleased the Father to give this kingdom to Christ's little flock (Lk 12:32).

If St Paul then had been asked the question, 'What must the apostle bring to the man of good will?', instead of answering, 'Nothing except assistance to come to himself,' he would have said, 'Everything, for Christ is all.'[1] The apostle must bring the man to Christ, for whom and by whom he already existed, and in whom he will finally be himself, beyond anything that he ever was. This had been St Paul's experience of conversion to Christ. As for the conclusions of the theory of anonymous christianity, at least as set out above, it scarcely seems that they have anything in common with St Paul's thought.

To say that salvation comes through the gospel is not to exclude men before Christ from salvation, leaving them in unbelief. But, instead of saying, 'they already possess salvation,' we shall say with the council that they are 'ordered' to it;[2] instead of saying that they *have* the

_____

dom of heaven? Evidently, the gift of the Holy Spirit . . . It is true that John the Baptist was great and of the highest virtue. In spite of this, he says to Christ: "I need to be baptised by you". You see, although as perfect as man can ever be, he asks to be reborn in the Holy Spirit' (In *Joh. ev.* v, 2, *PG* 73, col. 757).

[1] 'Do you perhaps think, what is the new thing that the Lord brought at his coming? You must know that what he has brought is all new, his person, promised in advance; what was announced in advance was precisely that the new reality would come to renew and revive man. For intelligent people at least the question no longer arises of what the King has brought new by comparison with those who announced his coming. For he has brought his person and made a gift to men of the good things promised' (Irenaeus, *Adv. Haer.*, IV, 34, 1. *PG* 7, coll 1083–1084).
[2] *The Church*, 16.

faith, we shall say with the council that, 'in ways known to himself, God can lead them to the faith.'[1]

All encounter Christ in death

The initial problem however remains: what are these ways? The early christians raised this problem too: what had become of their ancestors who had died before Christ? They never thought of finding the answer outside the gospel, but looked to an evangelisation by Christ himself in his death. Two texts of the First Epistle of St Peter speak of Christ's preaching to 'the spirits in prison' (3:18–20) and of 'the gospel preached to the dead' (4:6). The meaning of these texts is very much disputed; but the first christians were convinced, and expressed this in a variety of ways, that Christ in his

[1] *Missions*, 7. The interpretation of these two texts by the theologians of anonymous christianity is typical of their way of thinking. When the council says they are ordered to salvation, it means that they attain salvation; when it says that God can lead to faith those who have not been able to hear the gospel, this means that God *gives* them *the* faith from now on, in their state of ignorance. Cf K. Rahner, 'Das neue Bild der Kirche' in *Geist und Leben* 39 (1966), 11; *Theological Investigations*, VI, 390f.; 'The Teaching of the Second Vatican Council on Atheism' in *Concilium*, March 1967, 5–13.

This interpretation would be correct if, alongside salvation in its realisation and faith in its plenitude, there were only exclusion from salvation and absence of any faith. The distinction between christians and non-christians would be based on exclusion and everything belonging to the order of salvation would be on the same level. Karl Rahner writes in *Theological Investigations*, VI, 394: 'This means that the express revelation of the word in Christ is not something which comes to us from without as *entirely* strange, but *only* the explicitation of what we already are by grace' (our italics). Scriptural and patristic tradition speak of a preparation in grace making man already no stranger to Christ, but not yet one who has reached the stage of being 'in Christ'.

death met men who had lived before him and offered them salvation. Setting aside the over-colourful images in which it has been presented, this seems to be the simple, but rich theological import of the primitive faith in the 'descent into hell'.

Could not the problem of the ultimate salvation of men of today, living 'before' Christ, be solved likewise in the mystery of death, their own and that of Christ? *There is certainly no reason for excluding these men from the encounter with Christ in his 'descent into hell'.* In the glorifying death of Christ—descent of the Word into the depths of humanity and exaltation of man into the totality of God—the truth of the incarnation reaches its supreme and eternal affirmation. At that instant, Christ is extended to the two extreme poles of his mystery: he is totally 'consecrated and sent' (Jn 10:36), he is salvation effected and he is the one who comes to men. In his glorifying death, he is the centre to which all can gather and the point at which they are transformed into sons. Christ never encounters men except in his death and then it is in sharing his death. Baptism, eucharists and all the activities of his earthly life are for the christian simply so many ways of meeting Christ in participating in his death.

Beyond these means of salvation, however, the christian is aware of a fullness of participation with Christ in his death, in which the other deaths, brought about in baptism, eucharists and labours of charity, are 'completed': christian death, supreme sacrament of dying with another; 'if we have died with,' says St Paul, speaking of his physical death (2 Tim 2:11). How could physical death have this meaning for christians, unless Christ in his glorifying death became man's ultimate fullness, unless every man is created for him and at the term of his creation, that is, in his death—if he consents to this creative action—he is confronted by Christ?

Evangelisation on earth is this coming of Christ in his glorifying death, entering already into this world, the anticipation of this final encounter in death. Those who from now on enjoy the benefits of the gospel have no monopoly of final salvation; but in them the final reality, Christ in his glorifying death, is present within history. They have this privilege: *participation in the death of Christ in the present life, sharing in the world's redemption*, the privilege of a salvation already effected and of bringing this to others.

At the end of these reflections we may be permitted to return to this truth, too often forgotten: Christ's salvation is the final reality of history. Hence it is not effected from the beginning of history. Man, created in and for Christ, by the very fact of his first being, can be intended for salvation without being in the state of salvation. He gets there only by reaching the final term. And evangelisation is the means by which man can enter into communion with the final reality while he is still on earth.

Moreover, we may be permitted to point out an error of method that occurs too frequently. Theologians often distinguish by exclusion, although the realities of salvation are never distinguished from one another as mutually exclusive, but by a more or less close inclusion or—one might say—by a more or less intense communion with the centre, the final reality.

If this is admitted—that Christ is the final reality of history and that there are specific grades of participation in this reality—many aspects of christianity become clearer: first and foremost, that there is a true history of salvation and that men can be ordered to salvation without yet being christians.

8

EVANGELISATION BY PRESENCE*

Evangelisation is necessary; but what is evangelisation?
From the beginning (1 Thess 2:13), the church believed
that her preaching was the word of God. The attempt
has sometimes been made to justify this unheard of claim
by the charism that the church possesses of guarding the
word of God as once proclaimed and of transmitting it,
particularly as it is recorded in scripture. But an explanation of this kind amounts to a denial rather than a proof,
since it would mean that preaching transmits the word
of God but is not itself God's word.

In her preaching, the church still seeks to be Christ's
witness. The function of a witness is to attest what he
has seen. But we are now inclined to emphasise the
distance that separates the first apostles from the present-
day messengers of faith, to maintain that there is an
essential and complete difference between the two. It is
said that the apostles alone saw the events, the church
can only preserve and transmit their message. She herself therefore is not a witness.

Preserve and transmit! This sort of conception of
preaching is part of a whole theological system. According to a juridical theology of redemption, Christ once
acquired the merits of our redemption and these merits
are now applied, particularly in the sacraments. Just in
the same way, he once taught a doctrine and the church

* This chapter first appeared in *Wort in Welt. Festgabe für
Viktor Schürr*, Bergen-Enkheim 1968, 55–66.

now transmits it. At his death therefore Christ has left his church sacraments for the application of his merits and a faithful memory and a book—scripture—to preserve his message. And he himself has withdrawn from her.

But there is nothing in scripture about merits once acquired and now applied. It speaks of Christ who has himself become our salvation (1 Cor 1:30) and of our fellowship in Christ. In his paschal 'consecration' (Jn 17:19), Jesus is the Lamb of God that we have to eat so that our sins may be taken away; his flesh, sacrificed for the life of the world (Jn 6:51), is the bread which must be our food for eternal life; he is the vine of which we must become the branches. The salvation of each one— what is known in theology as subjective redemption—is achieved by sharing in objective redemption, that is, in the work of redemption as it is effected in Christ. The eucharistic celebration, in which the body of Christ is eaten in the event of his death and glorification, is the paradigm of the achievement of all subjective redemption.

Far from retiring from the world through death, Christ becomes more closely present to it than ever in the church. He does not die in order to leave, nor even to come back; he dies in order finally 'to come', by a universal presence and in the fullness of salvation: 'I will come to you' (Jn 14:18). He can be seen by men more than ever before: 'A little while and you will see me' (Jn 16:16). 'Jesus is the more clearly visible now that he is in the Father.'[1] By raising Christ, God effects salvation in him and at the same time offers to men this

[1] Ignatius of Antioch, *Romans* 3:3 (Translation S.P.CK., *Texts for Students*, London 1934, 30).

Christ who has become their salvation. The resurrection is incarnation in fullness: both total sanctification of Christ in God and total sending into the world (cf. Jn 10:36 and 17:18–19).

Christ did not merely leave his merits to the church to be distributed: he gives himself in the church, in fellowship. Likewise, he did not simply entrust the church with a gospel to be transmitted: *he became himself the gospel that she must preach.*[1] As St Paul puts it, 'the word', of which the church has the ministry, is nothing other than 'the mystery hidden for ages, . . . Christ in you' (Col 1:25–27). Christ is both salvation and the proclamation of salvation. As St John says, the word of God is the bread of life: this bread must be eaten in faith and it is Christ given for the life of the world (Jn 6). The eucharistic celebration, expressive sacrament of all subjective redemption, expresses first and foremost and in a very perfect way the mystery of evangelisation.

Preaching is not only at the service of a message once proclaimed and of a book; if this were all, it would be like the Old Testament ministry which St Paul calls the ministry of 'a written code', that is, of a lifeless document (2 Cor 3:6); on the contrary, it is 'the dispensation of the Spirit' (2 Cor 3:8), in the service of the Lord 'who comes' into this world and 'who is Spirit', the eternal reality, the fullness of salvation.

Faith is the effect of Christ's presence

If preaching did no more than transmit a message, it would not be adequate to the faith it is meant to rouse.

---

[1] 'Jesus Christ came not only to preach a Gospel but to *be* a Gospel' (Michael Ramsey, *The Resurrection of Christ*, London 1945, 8).

Scripture consistently describes the dead and risen Christ as the object of faith: 'We know that a man is not justified, . . . but through faith in Jesus Christ' (Gal 2:16). It is true that faith accepts also a doctrine that is taught and facts that are attested. But the doctrine is contained wholly and entirely in this first truth which is Christ, our salvation;[1] and the fact attested is nothing other than the effecting of salvation in Jesus Christ: 'If you believe in your heart that God raised him from the dead, you will be saved' (Rom 10:9). It was this faith in the salvation effected in his own person that the Christ of the synoptics tried to rouse, when he proclaimed the kingdom and identified this kingdom with that of the Son of God in his glory.

Believing therefore does not consist merely in giving an assent to words, to a doctrine and to attested facts; faith means possessing someone, an adherence to Christ. In the words of scripture, it consists in 'going to' Christ, 'submitting to' him, 'receiving' him, eating him as we eat bread. Faith effects a fellowship in Christ in which man is saved and of which the eucharistic communion is the expression (Jn 6). The believer attaches himself to Christ and commits himself to following him—'if any man would come after me'—in a total gift of self which goes as far as sharing in the Master's destiny: 'let him take up his cross and follow me' (Mk 8:34).

If the object of faith is someone, preaching cannot consist merely in transmitting words and attesting facts;

[1] In John 11:25–27 Jesus proposes a double object for faith: first, his person ('he who believes in *me*'); then a truth ('whoever lives and believes in me shall never die. Do you believe *this*?'). But this truth is itself included in the first object of faith: 'I am the resurrection.'

it must convey a presence. If the act of faith is the commitment of the whole person, faith will not be roused by a doctrine once revealed or by recalling facts that are behind us;[1] man commits his existence, his whole life, his whole future, only to a reality which is in front of him, which he can assimilate and in which he thinks he can find fulfilment. Man will never give his faith to Christ unless Christ comes today and reveals himself to him. Not that Christ has to reveal new truths today, since nothing can be added to the original revelation: 'The only Son, who is in the bosom of the Father, he has made him known' (Jn 1:18), once and for all.[2] But every one must be able to profit by the revelation of Christ made at the beginning, in order to enter with Christ into the fellowship of salvation. When the church first appeared, Christ was revealed to her so that she could begin to believe; he does not cease to reveal himself to her as she begins afresh—until the end—in each of her members, becoming a believer in each one of them.

Christian faith and human faith, therefore, are merely analogous. The latter means belief in facts attested by a witness, but without personal knowledge; christian faith also requires the mediation of a witness, but he must mediate a presence and an encounter, he must be the revelatory sign of the mystery he proclaims. This is how

---

[1] 'I cannot believe in a truth that is behind us' (J. Rostand, *Ce que je crois*, Paris, 1961 16). This great scholar thinks that christian truth is of such a kind, although in fact it is parousial, a truth to come, a future which becomes present and which man must assimilate.

[2] *Revelation*, 4: 'We now await no further new public revelation before the glorious manifestation of our Lord Jesus Christ', a revelation which is nothing other than Christ in his paschal mystery.

Christ on earth witnessed to himself (Jn 8:14, 18). In his earthly life he was the revelatory sign of his own mystery. Men of good will saw him and were brought within sight of the mystery, beyond the appearances at which the incredulous were held up: 'They have seen and have believed' (Jn 6:30, 36, 40; 20:29) and 'looked upon the word of life' (1 Jn 1:1).[1]

In christian faith there is an immediacy of perception, a personal grasp of the object of faith; the believer sees the mystery itself: 'We have beheld his glory, glory as of the only Son from the Father' (Jn 1:14). This glory of sonship, which Christ possesses because his Father begets him, is the object of faith and the evangelist claims to have seen it. He has likewise 'seen that the Father has sent his Son as the Saviour of the world' (1 Jn 4:14); this action is divine, it too is the object of faith and John has looked on it (cf Jn 5:37–38; 14: 9, 20). If this is faith, the proof that brings men to believe never lies merely in the knowledge and veracity of the witness, nor only in proofs external to the mystery proclaimed:[2] it lies in the mystery itself, in its revelation, in its appealing presence. 'When I am lifted up from the earth, I will draw all men to myself' (Jn 12:32), said Jesus, referring particularly to faith. If he appeals to his knowledge as a witness (Jn 3:11), it is still less a question of knowledge than of the divine mystery which comes into this world in his person (Jn 3:13). He may appeal to external proofs, but the essential proof is the

[1] In John 20:29 we read: 'Blessed are those who have not seen and yet believe.' Those are declared blessed then who believe without having seen with bodily eyes. But St John is aware of a real vision of faith, enjoyed by every believer.
[2] Miracles can rouse faith, but only in so far as they manifest the active presence of the mystery.

mystery which he is himself and which he proclaims (Jn 2:18–21; 6:30–32). 'Even though you do not believe me, believe the works', he declares (Jn 10:38; 14:11), testifying that, among other proofs, he is himself the essential proof. *The authority of the witness lies wholly and entirely in the mystery he proclaims.* For 'the light gives testimony to itself; it opens eyes that are healthy and is its own witness, so that the light may be known'.[1]

Thus faith is stimulated by the presence of the mystery and is directed to this presence.[2] Christ is not only the mystery proclaimed, he is the proclamation itself. St John calls him the *Logos* (the Word) of God, because all God's preaching to men is simply Christ coming in person. Preaching is Christ's parousia.

God evangelises the world by glorifying Christ

If Christ himself is God's word, who then can preach the gospel? Not all the human means of propaganda would suffice to make a single true believer. God alone can utter this word in the world, for he alone is the Father of Jesus Christ;[3] he alone can evangelise, he

[1] St Augustine, *In Joh. tract.* 35, 4, *CCL* 36, 319.
[2] Charity is possession of the presence; hope proceeds from an initial possession of the mystery towards its full possession. The word of the Church is a source of hope for the people of God, because it is the presence of the final reality in their midst. *If the word is not preached in its eschatological fullness, the people will be without hope.*
[3] St Augustine likewise makes Christ's preaching on earth go back to the generation of the Word. The words that Christ teaches, he has from the Father (Jn 14:24), whose begotten Word he is: 'Whatever the Father gives the Son, he gives by begetting him. For how otherwise would he give words to the Word, in whom he said all things ineffably?' *In Joh. tract.* 106, 7, *CCL* 36, 613. Cf *In Joh. tract.* 47, 14; 48, 6 and 9. *CCL* 36, 412, 415, 418.

alone can make believers, he who begets Jesus Christ
for men. St Paul, became a believer 'when God was
pleased *to reveal his Son' in him* (Gal 1:15–16).

Since the Father alone can rouse faith by sending and
revealing his Son, Jesus asks the Father to glorify him:
'Father, glorify thy Son that the Son may glorify thee'
and give life to all flesh, 'this . . . eternal life, that they
know thee and him whom thou hast sent' (Jn 17:1–3).
Already in John 3:14–16 Jesus had promised that his
exaltation would produce faith and fellowship in eternal life: 'The Son of man must be lifted up, that whoever believes in him may have eternal life.'

This is how Jesus on earth had already roused faith—
an initial faith—by the radiance of his being, by the
revelation of his glory: 'He manifested his glory; and his
disciples believed in him' (Jn 2:11). But during his life
on earth, his glory scarcely appeared, the mystery of sonship was not asserted in its fullness, the coming of Christ
was not yet complete. It is by raising him that God begets Jesus in the full glory of sonship: 'He has raised
Jesus, as it is written, . . . "Thou art my Son, today I
have begotten thee" ' (Acts 13:33); it is then that he is
appointed 'Son of God in power' (Rom 1:4), universal
Lord to whom the world submits in faith (Phil 2:9–11);
then that he sends him (Acts 3:26; 26:23) to proclaim
'the good news that what God promised to the fathers,
he has fulfilled' (13:32–33).

God evangelises the world by raising Jesus Christ,[1] the

[1] The Second Vatican Council expresses this in different
terms, saying that revelation is given especially in the death
and resurrection of Christ (*Revelation*, 2 and 4; *Religious
Freedom*, 11). Revelation is God's coming into this world,
expressed in words, events and persons, so that men may
enter into fellowship with him. This coming reaches its full-

good news is proclaimed by the divine action glorifying Christ. In his resurrection, Christ is preached and believed by men and he it is—in his resurrection—who is God's preaching to men, the cause of faith. The object of faith is also its source. Christian preaching therefore has deep roots: in the mystery of God, begetting Jesus Christ through the Holy Spirit (Rom 8:11) for men.[1] Faith exalts men very highly: it makes them recognise God in his supreme mystery as Father of Jesus Christ[2] and brings them into fellowship with Christ in so far as he is begotten by his Father; that is why he gives them 'power to become children of God' (Jn 1:12).

In a chapter of the Epistle to the Romans wholly and entirely devoted to faith, the apostle says that Christ 'was raised for our justification' (4:25), confirming the fact that it is in the resurrection that God evangelises the world. The traditional way of interpreting this text was to make the resurrection the great miracle, the firm motive of credibility, thanks to which man attains to faith and thus to justification. But this is not St Paul's idea. For him, the resurrection is not simply proof of the salvation merited by Christ: it is salvation itself, effected in Christ. For, in his resurrection, Jesus was 'justified in the Spirit' (1 Tim 3:16), became 'righteousness' and became this for us (1 Cor 1:30; 2 Cor 5:21), so that in him we are raised, justified in the spirit. God

---

ness in Jesus Christ, in his death and resurrection, and nothing more will ever be added to Christ, either to his death or to his resurrection.

[1] On the trinitarian origin of the apostolic mission, see *Missions*, 2–5.

[2] For St Paul, the revelation received on the Damascus road did not give him knowledge only of Christ, but still more deeply that of God, the Father of Jesus Christ.

saves us in the deed of redemption itself by the power of his action effecting salvation in Christ, raising him from the dead: 'He made us alive together with Christ' (Eph 2:5).

The resurrection is not merely an argument leading to faith and thereby to justification: it is an action with power to sanctify, *it produces the faith* in which man is justified. For 'christianity is not a work of persuasive eloquence, but of power'[1] (cf 1 Cor 2:4); it is divine creation by the power of God who raises Christ and thus creates believers, 'justified through faith in Jesus Christ' (Gal 2:16).

It must be repeated here: the resurrection of Christ is at the same time parousia, final salvation coming into the world. That is why Christ could contemplate in a single vision his paschal glorification and his parousia into the world: 'From now on you shall see the Son of man coming on the clouds of heaven '(Mt 26:64). This double aspect of the paschal mystery is reflected in the apostolic preaching: through it, God glorifies Christ in himself and offers him to men for their salvation. Preaching is not so much an apologia for Christ as his epiphany; it results from the action of divine power which raises Christ for men.[2] In this world, God raises Christ in the form of the kerygma,[3] in the form of evangelisation. By

[1] Ignatius of Antioch, *Romans* 3:3.
[2] J. Dupont, 'La parole de Dieu suivant saint Paul' in *La Parole de Dieu en Jésus-Christ*, Tournai, 1964[2], p. 72: 'The message of the resurrection prolongs the act by which God raised his Son.'
[3] This formula is used here in a sense different from that of Bultmann. The christian kerygma is something very different from the mere proclamation in the world of the saving death of Christ—for 'if Christ has not been raised, then our preaching is in vain' (1 Cor 15:14)—like the church as a whole, it is

a unique action, God himself raises him to the fullness of salvation, offers him to men by preaching, draws them into fellowship with him, justifies them in him in faith.

As an apostle, St Paul felt himself seized by the power of God raising Christ to lordship over the world and subjecting all thought to him in the obedience of faith (2 Cor 10:5; Rom 1:4–5). He calls himself 'apostle through the Father who raised Jesus Christ' (Gal 1:1); he knew that his message was a demonstration of this Spirit and of this power (1 Cor 2:4) in which Christ was raised (Rom 8:11; 2 Cor 13:4), and that his message was efficacious (1 Thess 2:13), producing in men the salvation that God achieved in Christ (Rom 1:16–17; 1 Cor 1:21; 15:1–2). That is why he calls this message 'word of God', for it is God who speaks thus to men by raising his Son for them. He calls it also 'the gospel of Christ' (Gal 1:7),[1] because it is nothing but Christ himself proclaimed to the world.

God evangelises the world by raising Jesus Christ in the church

Christ makes himself present to the world; but he does so by leaving it and by coming under other 'species'. He lives on a plane of existence different from that of men on this earth and is inaccessible to sense. He can be seen by them only under the signs of his presence.

The church is the primordial sacrament of this presence, the church which is the body of Christ (Eph 1:23;

---

the sacrament of the resurrection of Christ in this world. In its nominalist sense, Bultmann's formula is exegetically unacceptable.

[1] 'It is not simply a matter of the gospel which has Christ as its author, but of the gospel in which Christ proclaims himself.' H. Schlier, 'Der Brief an die Galater', coll. *Kritisch-exegetischer Kommentar über das NT.*, VII, Göttingen 1965, 39.

5:31–32), true presence and manifestation of the risen Christ to the world. It is only in her that Christ is raised *in this world*; in her is the point of contact of faith between Christ and men; she is the mediatrix of faith, because she is the body of Christ. Hence the state of faith in the world is dependent on the church: as she is faithful or not faithful, Christ is present or is not present to the world.

The apostolic mission of this church is concentrated in *the group of apostles* who are the beginning of the whole church (Eph 2:20) and her representatives. They cannot be content with spreading good tidings; they are preaching as they celebrate the eucharist when they 'proclaim the Lord's death until he comes' (1 Cor 11: 26) by making the Lord present, in his death and in his coming: celebrating the eucharist and proclaiming Christ to men, these are part of the same mission of rendering Christ present to men so that they may enter the fellowship of salvation with him. Whatever uncertainties may remain among exegetes about the primitive meaning of the apostolate, there seems no doubt that Jesus wanted to make the apostles his representatives. In St Paul's view, they represent him, not in a juridical fashion, but by bringing about his presence: they are the fragrance of Christ (2 Cor 2:15), the earthly procession of his eschatological triumph (2 Cor 2:14); they bear in their 'body the death of Jesus. . . . so that the life of Jesus may be manifested in (their) mortal flesh' (2 Cor 4:10–11); in their hearts shines 'the light of the knowledge of the glory of God in the face of Christ' (2 Cor 4:6); they place men before the crucified Christ who is the power of God (Gal 3:1; 1 Cor 1:23–24).

This mission is not reserved solely to those christians

who are more particularly the successors of the apostles. It is in their totality that christians constitute the church as body of Christ, sacrament of Christ's presence: all are part of the apostolic succession. As long as they are faithful, all possess this wonderful grace of being a sacrament of the coming of the Lord and of fellowship with him, as a eucharist celebrated among men in order to invite them to take part. Christians must give to the mystery they make present the name that reveals it, that of Jesus Christ. Christ's coming is revelation, of its nature directed to the word that expresses it; it is from human speech that Christ acquires his name—'the name by which he is called is The Word (utterance) of God' (Rev 19:13)—preaching is his nature. Moreover, every presence tries to find expression and strengthening in words, so as to be truly human, a presence to others and an entering into fellowship with them. *Christians therefore must preach also in words.*[1]

But it is not sufficient to speak: Christ must be made present and made known by talking about him. Christian language is a language, not only of information, but of communion. Words have this virtue, that through them a person expresses himself and goes out of himself, he is brought towards other men and himself acts in them with the aid of words. It is essential therefore for the christian to remain in Christ and for Christ to remain in him (Jn 15:5) and then the miracle is achieved: this man's word becomes Christ's word, the radiance of Christ's dynamic presence. There is no christian preaching without identification with Christ. If he does not remain in Christ, a christian is lying about God, even if much of what he says is true: for he is not expressing the

[1] Cf *Missions*, 20.

Truth, he is counterfeiting what the Father reveals to the world in begetting his Christ.

The true apostle 'speaks in Christ' (2 Cor 2:17) and on this account his word really is the word of Christ,[1] it springs from Christ and makes him present to men in the mystery of his death and resurrection,[2] producing in them faith and salvation (Rom 1:16). That is why preaching is itself in the image of Christ, a word crucified and charged with the power of the resurrection (1 Cor 1:17-18; 2:4): it bears the features of the mystery it conveys. The church can thus *bear witness* to Christ without having seen him with human eyes.

No doubt St Luke's conception of testimony would reserve the honour of witnessing to Christ's earthly companions (Acts 1:15-22). No doubt it is also true that there is no mission where there has been no sight: 'Am I not an apostle? Have I not seen Jesus our Lord' (1 Cor 9:1). It is the parousia that creates witnesses to Christ. On the Damascus road, St Paul enjoyed the

[1] The church preaches in the name of Christ, not only when she proclaims the word of scripture, but in all her preaching, so far as she is faithful to his grace. *Liturgy* 7 states; 'It is He (Christ) who speaks when the holy scriptures are read in the church.' But the first schema had: 'It is He who speaks when the holy scriptures are read and *explained* in the church.' It is regrettable that the intervention of some bishop or other prevented the retention of this text: it was in conformity with the thought of the New Testament. To remove any ambiguity it would have been sufficient to note that there is a difference between the word of scripture and the word of preaching, although both are derived from the charism the church possesses 'to speak in Christ' and in his Spirit.

[2] H. Schlier, 'La notion paulinienne de la parole de Dieu' in *Littérature et théologie pauliniennes*, Paris 1960, 135: 'In the word of God . . . every salvific event with all its benefits becomes present, at the same time as the person of the Saviour.'

vision of him who is called in the synoptics and in Acts 7:55 'Son of man', that is, Christ in his parousia.[1] But we all contemplate the Christ of glory; as St Paul says (2 Cor 3:18), in faith we all have sight of the coming Christ. St John too knew it. At a time when the last witnesses of the earthly life were gradually disappearing or had already disappeared, he asserted that others again have the right to bear witness: 'And we have seen and testify that the Father has sent his Son as the Saviour of the world' (1 Jn 4:14). This 'we', it seems, has an ecclesial dimension (cf also 1:1–3; 2:27; Jn 1:14): it refers not only to the author who writes this, but to all in the church who preach Christ.[2] What is essential to the apostolic testimony is outside sensible experience and accessible only to faith: except with the eyes of faith, no apostle saw Christ as Lord, Word of God, Saviour of the world, as the one whom the Father raises for eternal filial life. 'By asserting that it is a question (in the church's preaching) of eye-witnesses ('we have seen and testify'), the author underlines on the one hand the immediacy of experience—by faith—of the realities of salvation'[3] and on the other hand he extends to anyone who preaches Christ in a true faith the right to call himself an authentic witness. Every believer, at his own level, can say with Christ: 'We speak of what we know, and bear witness to what we have seen' (Jn 3:11). Faith is the source of the testimony: 'I believed, and so I spoke' (2 Cor 4:13).

This knowledge of faith makes the witness a sign of

[1] Cf L. Cerfaux, *Christ in the Theology of St Paul*, Edinburgh and London/New York 1959, 72.
[2] Cf E. Neuhaeusler, 'Zeugnis in der Schrift' in *Lexikon für Theologie und Kirche*, 1959², x, col. 1362.
[3] *Ibid.*

what he is attesting, As St Paul puts it, the apostle is
transfigured by his contemplation to resemble the
image of the Christ of glory (2 Cor 3:18). In St John
the vision of faith is 'an awareness, thanks to which
the whole existence of the person who knows is marked
by the object of his knowledge'.[1] For this knowledge is
like that which unites the Father and the Son (Jn
10:14–15), a comprehension through mutual presence
and possession (Jn 14:19–21); it permeates the christian
and transforms him into the mystery of Christ. Such a
witness can not only testify to what he has seen, *he becomes mediator of presence and vision and from then onwards it is
Christ who preaches Christ.*[2] It has been said that, according
to St John, the apostle is the transparency of Christ.[3]

[1] R. Bultmann, *Das Evangelium des Johannes*, Göttingen 1964[10],
290.
[2] This is an idea dear to St Augustine: 'Christ preaches
Christ. When the light reveals other things which are seen
in the light, does it need anything else to be revealed itself?
Light reveals everything and reveals itself' (*In Joh. tract.* 47,
3, *CCL* 36, 405–406). At the same time, St Augustine shows
that this revelation is given in the church which is identified
with Christ: 'Christ therefore preaches Christ, the body
preaches its head' (*Sermo* 354, 1. *PL* 39, col. 1563).
[3] J. Radermakers, 'Mission et apostolat dans l'évangile
johannique' in *Studia evangelica*, I, 120. *Texte und Untersuch-
ungen* 87, Berlin 1964. St Luke shows in his own way that the
witness is an image of Christ, when he describes St Stephen's
martyrdom on the lines of Christ's passion (Acts 7:55–60).
This conviction that the martyrs are an image of Christ is
found again throughout the early centuries. We read about
St Blandina that she 'was suspended on a stake and exposed
to be devoured by the wild beasts which were to attack her.
Her appearance, as if hanging on a cross, and her continual
prayers inspired the combatants with great zeal. In their
sister, in this conflict, they saw with their bodily eyes him
who was crucified for them' (Eusebius, *Ecclesiastical History*,
v, I, 41, *PG* 20, col. 425).

The scriptures constitute the church's preaching *par excellence*.[1] They are part of the paschal glorification of Jesus, of whom it is said, 'He (the Spirit) will glorify me' (Jn 16:14),[2] and it is through the paschal glorification that God sends and reveals his Son to men in the church. From the beginning, the scriptures were seen as a means of making Christ present and of fellowship

[1] Scripture and preaching are derived from one and the same charism of the Holy Spirit. As long as preaching is authentic, both are God's word addressed to the world in the church; in specifically distinct degrees, both are inspired by the Spirit of God and are means of contact with Christ, God's personal word. They cannot then be distinguished as separate entities, but as a full reality in its specific purity is distinguished from a reality of the same order that does not reach this fullness.

Since it is God's word in its specific purity, scripture is normative for all preaching: for a reality is normative within its order when it attains its specific purity. All the rest must be judged in the light of this exemplary plenitude. The church's preaching, although it is God's original word addressed today to the world, must never go outside this normative circle which is scripture properly understood: if it does, it is no longer God's word.

All that we have said in this way of preaching can be said of the church's living tradition, of which preaching forms part (cf *Revelation*, 8). Tradition has not the role solely of conserving and transmitting: although faithful to itself in its history, it is a reality that is always original; the church likewise, founded in the past, is in Christ always at its primary source. Scripture and tradition are not two separate realities (cf *Revelation*, 9–10), for scripture is the church's living tradition and—on its side—tradition shares in the privilege of scripture of being God's word. Tradition, while it is being developed and unceasingly adapted to history, must remain faithful to scripture which is this tradition in its specific purity.

[2] The gospel according to St John particularly seeks to be this glorification of Christ by the Spirit (cf. F. Mussner, *The Historical Jesus in the Gospel of St John*, London and Freiburg 1967, 64–67.

with him; they have been compared—those of the Old Testament also which are read in church—to the meal of the body and blood of Christ;[1] and they have been understood as a way of creating an immediate contact of faith between man and God.[2] In order to be thus word of God and presence of Christ to the world, the scriptures must be read in the church: for there alone God preaches Christ, there he sends him into this world.

Baptism was regarded in the primitive church as the kerygma incorporated in an action.[3] It was seen as the sacrament of faith, not merely because it can be received only in faith, but because it produces faith: baptism is 'the water of faith'[4] which produces true believers.[5] Does not faith consist in going to Christ and clinging to him by sharing in his mystery of salvation? Now, it is in the reception of baptism that the movement of faith carrying man towards Christ is completed (Rom 6:3; Gal 3:27) and that this fellowship of death and resurrection is also established (Col 2:12). Baptism thus demonstrates that faith is brought about by the means which make us present to Christ and in contact with him.

Among the sacraments, the eucharist is word of God and 'sacrament of faith' *par excellence*, it is 'the apex of the whole work of preaching the gospel'.[6] It is the eucharist especially that produces the permanent miracle of a church which believes in Jesus Christ in the midst of

[1] 'Drink both cups of the Old and the New Testament, for in both you drink Christ' (St Ambrose, *Exp. Ps* 1:33, *PL* 14, col. 940). Cf *Revelation*, 21 and 26.

[2] St Thomas, *In Ep. II ad Tim.*, c.3, 1.3.

[3] Cf L. Villette, *Foi et Sacrement*, vol. I, *Du Nouveau Testament à saint Augustin*, Paris 1959, 30 and 100.

[4] *Aqua fidelis* (St Cyprian, Ep. 63, 9. *CSEL* 3B, 707).

[5] L. Villette, *op. cit.*, 46–53; 111–112; 180–191; 271–279.

[6] *Priests*, 5.

the world's unbelief. It is the apex, not only because of its kerygmatic and catechetical values, but because she is *par excellence* the sacrament of the presence of Christ in the world.

It seems possible therefore to state as a universal law: *it is by Christ's presence that men are evangelised.*[1] In order to be a source of faith, the church must take care to be the radiant presence of Christ among men.[2]

Christ's mode of presence in evangelisation

The fact is certain, but the nature of this presence is difficult to determine. First of all the question arises: *how is Christ present to men in preaching?*

Christ promised his presence to the church; but it is a presence which, until the end, will be that of someone who is to come: 'I go away, and I will come' (John 14:28), a presence which is at the same time an approach. As St Paul puts it, believers have been transferred into the kingdom of light (Col 1:13) and live in the full light of day (Rom 13:13; Eph 5:8), and yet the Lord is merely close (Phil 4:5). The eucharist, too, is presence and coming; it satisfies but at the same time rouses desire: an annunciatory presence and a promise. For the risen Christ is the *ultimate* fullness of this world; he can never be present in the fashion of this world's realities, but as fullness towards which man must set

---

[1] *Missions*, 9: 'By the preaching of the word and by the celebration of the sacraments, whose center and summit is the most holy Eucharist, missionary activity brings about the presence of Christ, the Author of salvation.'
[2] Another conclusion is also forced upon us: to remain in the faith, the encounter with Christ must be maintained, by living membership of the church, by the sacraments and by prayer.

out. Such is preaching: it introduces into earthly time the risen Christ who, although present through preaching, is the world's final reality, placed at the end of the road and towards which men must proceed by faith.

The question raised is part of a vast problem, always relevant throughout the church's history: that of the final parousia or—in other words—of the proximity of the parousia of which scripture so often speaks. The imperfection of Christ's presence by preaching does not lie in the fact of Christ, for in him the fullness of the mystery of the parousia is realised from the time of the paschal glorification. The imperfection is in man who is to be saved, to whom the preaching is addressed and for whom the eschatological Christ is present in the form of a goal that leads him on. For the unbeliever he is absent, as light is absent for the blind.[1]

The imperfection lies also in the preaching, for Christ is preached in an earthly church in which he is present to men to the extent that the church is united to him. In her visible reality, the church can be the sign only of his hidden presence and the road towards this presence. Because christians are often lacking in fidelity, the sign is often obscure and the road difficult. Because of this double imperfection, man must set out on the road in order to encounter through preaching the Christ who is nevertheless present to him. He must 'go to Christ', he must believe. He will not do this of himself, the Father must draw him (Jn 6:44; Acts 16:14). God exercises this attraction by means of Christ: 'Does not Christ attract, revealed by the Father?'[2] Man is drawn to Christ

[1] Cf St Augustine, In Joh. tract., 35, 4, CCL 36, 319.
[2] St Augustine, In Joh. tract., 26, 5, CCL 36, 262. 'It is this revelation which attracts' (ibid.).

only if he sees him, it is the sight of the 'true bread' that rouses this hunger.[1] This hunger is roused in the heart of every good man when Christ in his truth appears to him. For man permits himself to be drawn by truth, permits himself to be drawn by justice, by happiness, by eternal life, and 'Christ is all that',[2] since he is the fullness of all. The apostle must not too readily attribute the failure of the world to men's evil will: he must be careful himself to remain faithful, so that the splendour and attraction of the face of Christ may appear in him.[3] And this splendour is the splendour of love.

A second question arises: *how is Christ present through those who preach?* This question too is part of a vaster problem: that of the identification of the church with Christ. For our purpose, it is sufficient to note that Christ does not become present through the church and the apostles as in impersonal signs, such as bread and wine in the eucharist. The church is the body of Christ and therefore apostolic through a union of faith and love with Christ (Jn 14:20; Eph 3:17) and through sharing in his paschal mystery. She is the body of Christ, his presence in the world, to the extent to which she is the loving and believing bride. Preaching therefore is something very personal: the church preaches, is the word of God, only because of her union with God. For redemption as a whole is a personal work. It is so in Christ who, in his death and resurrection, is himself salvation; it is

[1] St Augustine, *In Joh. tract.*, 26, 4, *CCL* 36, 261: 'There is joy in the heart of him for whom this heavenly bread is sweet.'
[2] *Ibid.*
[3] 'Message to Humanity', issued at the opening of the Second Vatican Council (Abbott, *Documents*, 4): 'May the church, pastors and flocks, radiate before all men the lovable features of Jesus Christ.' Cf *Church in the Modern World*, 21, 5; 43, 6.

so in the church which shares in salvation through fellowship with Christ in his death and resurrection. God produces in Christ the fruits of redemption like ears born from the grain of wheat and in the apostles like grapes that ripen on a vine. Such are the fruits of preaching.

Hence, to be an apostle, it is not sufficient to have received the sacraments of the apostolate; baptism, confirmation, holy orders, are never more than sacraments of initiation and, when they have been received, it is still necessary to become an apostle. St Paul tells christians, 'you have put on Christ' (Gal 3:27), and charges them: 'Put on Christ' (Rom 13:14; Col 3:1–10).

Christ alone is the revelation of Christ. He is preached by men who are united with him to the point of being his presence among men.

INDEX

INDEX OF BIBLICAL REFERENCES